Out of Ur

Also by Rochelle Owens

Poetry
Not Be Essence That Cannot Be
Four Young Lady Poets
Salt & Core
I Am the Babe of Joseph Stalin's Daughter
The Joe 82 Creation Poems
The Joe Chronicles Part 2
Shemuel
Constructs
W.C. Fields in French Light
How Much Paint Does the Painting Need
Rubbed Stones and Other Poems
New and Selected Poems: 1961-1996
Luca: Discourse on Life and Death
Triptych
Solitary Workwoman

Plays
Futz and What Came After
The Karl Marx Play and Others
The Widow And The Colonel
Futz and Who Do You Want Peire Vidal?
Plays by Rochelle Owens

Fiction
Journey to Purity

Editor
Spontaneous Combustion: Eight New American Plays

Translation (French)
The Passersby, by Liliane Atlan

Film
Futz

Video
Oklahoma Too
How Much Paint Does the Painting Need
Black Chalk

Out of Ur

New & Selected Poems
1961–2012

Rochelle Owens

Shearsman Books

First published in the United Kingdom in 2013 by
Shearsman Books
50 Westons Hill Drive
Emersons Green
BRISTOL
BS16 7DF

Shearsman Books Ltd Registered Office
30–31 St. James Place, Mangotsfield, Bristol BS16 9JB
(this address not for correspondence)

www.shearsman.com

ISBN 978-1-84861-258-7

Acknowledgements

Some of these poems have appeared in the following journals and anthologies: *Abacus*, *America a Prophecy*, *An Active Anthology*, *Another Chicago Magazine*, *A Big Jewish Book*, *Boundary 2*, *Broadway Boogie: A Century in Two Decades*, *The Café Review*, *The Coldspring Journal*, *Confrontation*, *Connections*, *Contact II*, *A Controversy of Poets*, *Damascus Road*, *Deep Down*, *First Intensity*, *Four Young Lady Poets*, *Golden Handcuffs Review*, *Intrepid*, *The Iowa Review*, *Jacket2*, *Moody Street Irregulars*, *The New Verse News*, *New Wilderness Letter*, *The New York Quarterly*, *Nimrod*, *No More Masks*, *Objects*, *Open Places*, *Open Poetry*, *The Partisan Review*, *Poems and Poetics*, *Poems for the Millennium* (vol. 2), *Poetry Now*, *Poets On*, *Postmodern Culture*, *Psyche*, *Rising Tides*, *Shell*, *Six Pack*, *Some/Thing*, *Stations*, *Stooge*, *Sulfur*, *Sun*, *Talisman*, *Temblor*, *Texture*, *13th Moon*, *Tree*, *Trobar*, *2 plus 2*, *Unmuzzled Ox*, *Upstairs at Duroc*, *Yugen*, and *Zone*.

The author wishes to express her gratitude to the following publishers: Trobar Books for *Not Be Essence That Cannot Be*, Black Sparrow Press for *Salt & Core* and *The Joe 82 Creation Poems*, Kulchur Foundation for *I Am The Babe of Joseph Stalin's Daughter*, and *How Much Paint Does the Painting Need*, New Rivers Press for *Shemuel*, Poetry Around for *Constructs*, and Contact II Publications for *W.C. Fields in French Light*. Parts of *The Joe 82 Creation Poems* were originally published in 1973 by Burning Deck as *Poems from Joe's Garage*; parts of *W.C. Fields in French Light* were originally published in 1984 as *French Light* by The Press with the Flexible Voice.

Contents

for George, always

New Poems

(2006–2012)

Song from Out of Ur

Speak to a configuration of stains
even a silk shirt of the man from Marrakech
even a configuration of stains will be
made to speak sublime yellow-green
smears of avocado pulp the man from
Marrakech enemies at his feet the son
of a Macedonian his peach porcelain chin
its cleft pierced by a thorn pierced
is the man from Marrakech the son of a
Macedonian he crouches over a vanity sink
dappled with mother-of-pearl bearing
the weight of a nightmare a nightmare
about iron stairs about a long row
of embryos luminous organs fibrous pits
Narcissus purging
jabbing his two-inch pinky nail evil it feels
into the cleft of his chin
a levantine hook on a rampage
from out of Ur into the hotel his private
quarters red hot mosaic tiles hooks for
every hang-up made by master craftsmen
the man from Marrakech
eyes of pale gray-green pale gray-green eyes
son of a Macedonian
mummified is his code of honor

In ancient Phoenicia
a woman holds a sublime yellow-green
fabric smeared with avocado pulp
years later her unmarried hump-backed
son will unfold the cloth
Even a configuration of stains
will be made to speak

*

An urge for rhythms of Marrakech
gilded the row of upper teeth of the school master
listening to American jazz smiling at a man
from Sudan an engineer wearing a necklace
and a diamond stud in his ear
The man from Marrakech rises from the
Greek revival chair feeling the rays of the sun
resurrecting the dead

The false door of lust opens
frustrates and disappoints
famous the false door of lust
slamming the head breaking the nose
cracking the jaw splitting the gums ejecting
the gilded row of upper teeth teeth
of Cavafy Donatello Passolini Versace
short dark solid men mavericks
with spleens of hot lava
orbiting the mediterranean sun

*

A djellaba is a djellaba is a robe a robe of roses
sings the man from Marrakech
letting fall around his ankles purple roses
the djellaba its distinct parts is like a fluid
a fluid of roses is a chemical analysis—proof
le bien et le mal
drop by drop its sound distinct
le bien et le mal
And he sings to pierced nipples nipples
on the sculptured torso—a man from Sudan
And when he sings the words
the words are pigment cells vegetal to vegetal
cooling the skin the words are hairs
pushing through layers pushing through
layers of skin scalp armpit bones in a sac
words of a song from out of Ur from out of Ur
from out of the throat of the man
from Marrakech

*

The children always crawl to golden coins
golden coins draw the children
whispers the man from Marrakech
And he grants wishes to a man from Sudan
and desire breaks its molten outer core
then drawing upon his economic advantage
whispers I am the Alpha and Omega
world without end

*

In the picturesque Medina
two old men are trading photos
cruise ships voyaging to America
Inside a galaxy a cloud of dust and gas
gas and dust inside a galaxy
Two old men are smoking water pipes
in the picturesque Medina
two old men are playing cards talking politics
sipping coffee
hearing the call to prayer
the man from Sudan an engineer
wearing a necklace
and a diamond stud in his ear
the man from Marrakech
eyes of pale gray-green pale gray-green eyes
son of a Macedonian
an athlete whose stamina was tested
with javelin hammer and discus
smiling and remembering a silk shirt
smeared with avocado pulp
hammer and discus are thrown
and the weight of the athlete
spirals in as dense as a star

*

Come see what has been called
the poignant picture—a father bearing
twin sons in his arms—poignant the chanting
aramaic words and they were born
from frozen embryos
Forced deeper the weight of a dream
about a gold ostrich egg and shining through
the shell the form that you should put
your money into—a two-headed child
two pairs of pale gray-green eyes
colors and patterns of the iris painted
with a fine sable brush
And dread is a light transparent veil
over the eyes of the man from Marrakech
smoking a water pipe eating sleeping reading
playing computer games
then feeling for his wallet for the accordian-fold
interior credit cards driver's license bills
receipts coins and photos
of the winged cherubim their halos
glittering circling red orange yellow
the young always crawl to golden coins
then chanting in aramaic a prayer
'And they are the winged cherubim
with the faces of children'

The Glacier

For a thousand years the glacier
expanding outward outward from the walls
of a dead artist's garden in Tuscany—
a hallucination of an obscure poet
living alone in Angola
writing in Portuguese

'Green the gardens of Tuscany'

the word 'avore' tattood on her forehead
snow forming ice
the glacier expanding outward outward
moving slowly slowly
lumps of ice tilting twisting
rows of words order of words

'Green the gardens of Tuscany'

parts of words
the word 'abandon' stuck in her throat
lovely the letters like roots
spirals of roots multicellular
slender pliant twigs
lovely the letters like arteries

'Green the gardens of Tuscany'

interlacing shapes colors wind rivers
blood of her mammalian brain
flowing outward outward
forming pictures of hieroglyphs
a honeycomb candles metal glass
an elephant gothic script
the mouth of a fish

'Green the gardens of Tuscany'

leather bound books crop dusters
the mass of ice moving downward
the glacier flowing cresting
sound and meaning breaking break
ing rocks and ice
lovely the letters like the spine
of the aardvark bending

'Green the gardens of Tuscany'

her mammalian brain
expanding outward outward
forming rows of letters
order of letters
parts of words rushing darting
stinging jellyfish
the debris of words from wind and fire

'Green the gardens of Tuscany'

solid liquid and gas
chunks of stone and iron
the letters cooling gleaming dimming
the word 'abandon' stuck in her throat
letters orbiting her head
fusing into words
giant storms of letters spiraling
the glacier expanding outward outward

Eye of the Botanist

In memory of Joy Walsh and Theodore Enslin

Amid the sameness he blinks going out
feeling in front
of his face

and landing on his right eyelid
sunlight blood vessels
a seed of the larkspur

under the eyelid
a seed of the larkspur
under the eyelid

the hind toe of a lark
scratching the cornea
stinging lacerating penetrating

a seed of the flower
blue color is the larkspur
the eye of the beholder

a fireball e x p l o d i n g
the eye of the botanist
a dwelling

the universe e x p a n d i n g
amorous the greedy seed amorous
the greedy seed

a uterus its sweet nest
a triumph of genus desiring
desiring to fecundate

be fruitful and multiply
a seed of the larkspur flowering
s p r e a d i n g

the eye of the botanist e x p a n d i n g
the grandeur of the cornea
Jesus saying—

suffer the larkspur children
beautiful children
luring the hummingbirds and bees

joyous the seed of the larkspur
in the heat of summer
joyous the song of the lark

glorious the eye of a botanist
lit with flaming torches

Horishi

Desiring e u p h o r i a
envying Van Gogh the tattoo artist
begins carving sunflowers

a layer of s k i n the s k i n
the c a n v a s
absorbing sunlight

s p a c i n g the petals
each puncture the molten eyeballs
thumbs and fingers of Van Gogh

marking the s k i n
inserting the pigment
the s k i n the c a n v a s

absorbing sunlight
each leaf touches of yellow
dabs of white and green

a single rapid stroke

ravenous the flesh the c a n v a s
near the armpits
among the petals of flowers

a bright blue halo
leaves of beaten gold from the sun's core
the mystical signature of Van Gogh

hidden inside of the thighs
of the samurai warrior
occult words energy of the Logos

from ink to blood
the thorns piercing the s k i n
the c a n v a s absorbing sunlight

the sound needles make the waves
the waves and wind

Ode to a Gila Monster

There goes a Gila monster
in the beginning
of the triumphant twenty-first century
there goes a Gila reptile
following soundlessly
soundlessly following
is a Gila monster a mute animal
a monster of brilliant color
there goes a Gila reptile
studded with yellow and black
beadlike tubercles
there goes a beautiful reptile
with lidless eyes
devoid of dread and shame
in harmony with the microscopic algae
in harmony with a zygote in a moist habitat
in harmony with a basil plant
in harmony with fern and poison mushroom
there goes a cold-blooded Gila monster
a cold-blooded messenger
an ingenious reptile
seeking and smelling insects fruit rodents
the aromatic plants
in harmony with hibiscus and sand dunes
in harmony with chemical molecules
with amphibians and their larvae
with layers of water
in harmony with jellyfish corals and seaworms
with giant redwood trees
in harmony with mammals scorpions fish
crustaceans and turtles
in harmony with layers of water
in harmony with symmetry with layers of water
in harmony with Alpha and Omega
in harmony with the rays of the sun

*

In front of a
carved wood sculpture
in the violet light
Mary Magdalene Mary Magdalene
In the violet light
there goes a Gila monster
a Gila monster
majestically formed
a monster of gorgeous color
her body an astrological plan
studded with yellow and black
beadlike tubercles
like atoms locked into a pattern
vibrating particles
dabs of orange blue and green
forming an image in
the violet light
light rays entering the eyes
of a Gila monster
her body sovereign of
stems branches roots plants
of bones flesh blood vessels
sovereign of the wood sculpture
of the long slender limbs
delicately modeled hands
and feet carved with a chisel
Mary Magdalene cut from cut
from a single length of poplar
her hair highlighted with gold leaf
strands of her hair blowing
blowing across the lidless eyes
eyes of a Gila monster

*

Naming a wish wishing a name
Gila monster descended
into this world
triumphant

in the twenty-first century
hatched from the egg of the sky
emerging from a fiction
her body an astrological plan
in harmony with the rays
of the sun
slowly slowly slowly slowly
towards the four directions
a monster
of brilliant color
sleeping underground
dreaming of monkey cup
and cobra lily
vulnerable flesh eater
spiritual carnivore
Gila monster
the warmest of mothers
like the warmest of mothers
righteous and paradoxical
vulnerable flesh eater
spiritual carnivore
there goes a beautiful reptile
slowly slowly slowly slowly
towards the four directions
a cold blooded messenger
a monster
of brilliant color
her fatty tail
studded with yellow and black
beadlike tubercles
her gift of spit
her healing reptile spit
spit of power spit of cure
spit of metamorphosis
in harmony with layers of water
in harmony with Alpha and Omega
in harmony
with the rays of the sun

*

When as an incarnation
mother of the milky way
in the triumphant twenty-first century
O monster of harmonies
flying descending
into this world
descending
O Gila monster O virgin queen
imperial reptile
hatched from the egg of the sky
flying Gila
descending into this world
around her a spreading hibiscus
O philosopher with lidless eyes
all-seeing
eternal wunderkind
devoid of dread and shame
O head and fatty tail
majestically formed with yellow
and black beadlike tubercles
pure as alabaster shining gold
mother of the milky way
of metamorphosis
her gift of spit
her healing reptile spit
spit of power spit of cure
vulnerable flesh eater
spiritual carnivore
wafting incense sanctifying
the four directions
slowly slowly slowly slowly
scuttling over the sand
a cold blooded messenger
a monster of rapture
in harmony
with the rays of the sun

Woman from Tibet

There was once a woman from Tibet
who paid the rent and electric bill
flaying carcasses in the Market Place
Bones of a bird's wing
hinged together
The pants she wore
were made of burlap and silk
and the edges were frayed
Bones of a bird's wing
hinged together
Watching the woman from Tibet
earn her living was as good as any
blood sport
Bones of a bird's wing
hinged together
Hidden in the pockets of her pants
were four lapis lazuli rings
tied together with a string
Bones of a bird's wing
hinged together
Work is a binding obligation—
You must flay carcasses
in the Market Place
Bones of a bird's wing
hinged together
Living in the fiction of her glass eye
the gouged out one of the past
the woman from Tibet flays carcasses
Bones of a bird's wing
hinged together

*

Words from bones the woman from Tibet
her hard skeleton her animal soul
pouring into your blood
Tibetan words words moving up and down

felt in your spine your fibrous substance
Moving her lips
the woman from Tibet
standing in front of a camera
in the fiction of its glass eye
living in the fiction
the gouged out one of the past
Work is a binding
obligation—
You must flay carcasses
in the Market Place
as good as any blood sport
rows of birds rows of knives
FLESH becomes WORD through your teeth
your eyebrows through your skull
your brain your nasal bones
in your muscles
Moving her lips
words in Tibetan spiraling etching
onto your corneas
turquoise glass lapis lazuli words
embedded into the knives
the blades vibrating
circling white lights circling
through your auditory canal
felt on the palms of your hands
soles of your feet
through your heart
The woman from Tibet
standing in front of a camera
in the fiction of its glass eye
living in the fiction
the gouged out one of the past
Work is a binding
obligation—
You must flay carcasses
in the Market Place

Death Rattles Gauguin

When you are hearing Tahitian
speaking through fingers shaping fingers
forming a hole a circle a spiral
a hemisphere a terrain
then an island
                                        The shape of a woman
                                                    out of a corner
                                                              of your eye
A woman with purple blossoms
in her braided hair and on her head a basket
filled with dried husks of fruit shells
teeth and finger bones the dry bones
give out faint light
                                        The muscles of her neck
                                                    tropical orchids
                                                              twined around
your brain—the final domain—vibrations of air
the death rattle of Gauguin a hollow tube
filling with pigment O islands of epidermis
deep ridges of malachite layer by layer
layer by layer the skin
breaking down vascular tissue
pumping stomach gut bladder pancreas
intestine anus
                                        luminous membranes
                                                    blood in blood out
                                                              organs liquefying
And in a single rapid stroke swarming insects
like star clusters—a colony of fungus gnats
lay their soft eggs
The skull filling up with blue-green algae
with the sea and air the skull of Gauguin
filling with strumming plucking sounds
filling with the sounds of Tahitian
The dry bones give out faint light

Goethe as a Foetus

A poem for nefarious times is a knot
not a definite form in these
evil days
only a different shape
for deplorable uses
And the knot's refusal of self-definition
makes it an inescapable master
in these evil days
and the poem like the knot
like the knot is always seizing seizing

Here are eight imaginary views of a world
without poets
A scorpion indifferent to shock waves
Sharp blades of a lawnmower
A shark without its fins
Storms of swirling plastic particles
A cell phone landing on a rock
A voice without a turtle
No shaman incantation
And Goethe as a foetus
flushed
from his mutter's uterus

Sovereignty

The matchmaker says a body is its parts

Ever on the surface appears a story
of Iberian days a state of mind
white sand from end to end
explaining the surface of the skin

A naked martyr standing pigeon-toed
opens her right hand pale yellow
the sand in the hollow of her palm
the shade expanding

A space between words étoile horseshoe
evil-eye taliswoman

And power a conjurer and truth a fissure
darkening yellowing on the bottom
of her left foot

*

A woman says a word that you know
her high cheekbones cut from a red stone
a red stone sought by a global market
trafficking in human kidneys

And an index
finger waves a finger waves for it is
a versatile tool uniquely capable

A woman says a word that you know
that you know

From the earth's crust
plant material and blood

And blood is cleansed in the fist-sized bean-shape
A woman says a word that you know
that you know

A brain cut out from the skull of a woman
her high cheekbones cut from a red stone

A typhoon the head-butting rains
gaps in the sequence of events laid down
and eroded away

*

Away from the traffic and pointing at
a hypothetical male a woman says a word
with a smile while her key ring slips off
slips off an index finger and before
another theft another theft in Calcutta gaps
in the sequence of events
sequence of events a marriage between
pauper and wealthy woman from Delhi

And naught but sovereignty says a word
a word that you know

On the earth's surface
seven continents rivers and deserts
the flexible long neck of a woman stretches
and an index finger waves spiraling bands
of wind and rain and strong little legs
of a pauper run little legs of a pauper run

Escape to spring from one continent to
another

And a sign says "keep out" those
who will not dance to a tune of their misery
to a tune of their pain their pain as perfect
as tubular bells tam tam gongs and sitars

to be no more of this story cut out of the
middle this story of Iberian days
And naught but sovereignty says a word
a word that you know dividing itself
into head inchoate eyes and ears
ears that grind up sound

For the word –theft– is sound ground up
becoming a gift and it is a gift of a red stone
a red stone in a bean-shape
and the size of a fist

And beauty is the arch beauty is the arch
of the foot of a pauper

*

The operating room and lights that beam
scan across the screen are the eyes and eyes
are organs of wonder wondrous organs

And the two eyeballs set in bony sockets
Behold the gift!

The gift of a red stone in a bean-shape
precious the intact skeleton precious the skull
spine bones joints the form of the human body

And naught but sovereignty is the matchmaker
naught but sovereignty says a body is its parts
knowing which side his bread is buttered—
as a surgeon on a safari
or a trip around the world

Behold the bread of Kali!—an abundance
of paupers paupers of inchoate eyes rattling
spiral seashells jingling bracelets

They are called the bread of Kali
because Kali devours them
And they are deaf from birth
they are the deaf paupers deaf to the flutes
deaf to the sitars deaf to the tam tam gongs
deaf to the tubular bells

*

The paupers ears are drawn
with a quill-point a beautiful form
a calligraphy that is a curved stroke
like the letter C and the C multiplies
becoming cumulus clouds
and paupers ears

The paupers ears are pale yellow silk
sliding through henna stained fingers
of the wealthy woman from Delhi
whose gift to her son her only
son is a gift

A gift of a red stone
bought from a global market
trafficking in human kidneys
whose only son
has the dark blue skin of Siva

And Siva wears a rugby shirt
racing his chariot contracting his biceps
his skin mild moist racing his chariot
a bronze Hummer

A gift from the wealthy woman from Delhi
her pale yellow sari a glowing streak of light
layers of silk winding winding
around Kali's waist
cascading down
becoming cumulus clouds

and paupers ears
her bloody thumbs
and index fingers knot and tuck
cumulus clouds and paupers ears

And swirling around Kali's feet and toes
light rays of sovereignty

Sovereignty under the skin
fat muscle and bone

Sovereignty is a cutting tool
mass-produced like the toy monkeys
like rattling spiral seashells

The jingling bangles
of the deaf paupers the flutes sitars
the tam tam gongs

Out of the Digital Age

Hearing that an actor
dying after falling
despairing over his balancing act
falling off a metal stool
changing a light bulb
shattering his glass skull

Applauding the audience viciously and hypocritically
casts lots for his robe
a drunken slumming suburban crowd
women and men garbed
in opulent fur coats sable mink chinchilla
trafficked leopard

From out of the digital age come the entertainers two by two
also three by three they come
also four by four they come
comedians riffing on politics
jeering at the religious
monotheist pantheist and atheist idealists
ogling small boys with blissful faces
gyrating in spandex and leather
little girls smiling and pivoting
pivoting on crocodile stiletto heels
male and female wrestlers
preening laughing and cracking whips

From out of the digital age come the politicians celebrities
profiteers
also the moral and depraved
they come also

And in the actor's dying brain—
Behold!—a triptych a single image
a fetal skull sprouting tooth-buds
a pelvis riddled with arthritis
light shining through the porous bones

An old man with a pink face his sequin dress glinting
under a fat lustrous brown mink
bidding on an illuminated manuscript
and a python wallet
the dead actor's delusions
etched into the skin
his obsolete convictions stitched
into the seams
obscure details of dying a poetics of Space and Body

You feel your skull and spine shrinking inside the skin
your wrathful hands
tearing up prehistoric forests
you hear volcanic gases

The dead actor's windpipe filling with vibrating words
his neck twisting to the side
and bleeding into his brain a thousand images
fish insects mammals
turtles crustaceans
a dense montage of broken stage props
bleeding into his brain

Priestly Litany

When the world's
most trusted deceptions
like a parasitic plant
its mouth parts opening closing
Oh song of green leaves and stems
its mouth parts closing opening
Oh song of moisture and tears
of mucus membranes and canker sores
Oh forgiving child of my animal soul
Oh bleeding child
of my effervescent blood
Your blood is the blood of the Lamb

Sweet deaf boys donkey boys
monkey girls
little lambs of the Unholy See
lambs of ME and MY body
Your blood is the blood of the Lamb

Oh hovering winged creatures
Behold the Lord's Supper
under sacramental robes
Your blood is the blood of the Lamb

Oh grasping thirsty angels
angels of vengeance and repentance
angels of muteness and the Holy Secret
sweet deaf boys
Your blood is the blood of the Lamb

For the sake of my sorrowful passion
for the sake of my effervescent blood
for the sake of my spasm and orgasm
for the sake of my salt and vinegar
Your blood is the blood of the Lamb

For the sake of my ecstasy
and giggling rapture
for the sake of your Holy Rape
and sphincter muscle
for the sake of my Animal Soul
Oh forgiving child
Your blood is the blood of the Lamb

Chomsky Grilling Linguica

PREFACE

Professor Chomsky's body of political discourse is his engagement with the world. The poem is an act of intervention upon the body of Professor Chomsky, its form and content dictated by the subject of Professor Chomsky as a living, breathing body prospering in a beautiful, pristine Cape Cod seaside town. Not only natural resources, earth, sky and water, but also visible and invisible species and forces become integrated with the man who is Professor Chomsky and augment his physical and metaphysical being.

I was at a dinner party a dinner party I was
invited to the house the house of the famous American
linguist Noam Chomsky I was at a Chomsky dinner party
a party given by Chomsky a Chomsky dinner party Chomsky was
grilling chunks grilling chunks chunks
of Portuguese chunks of Portuguese sausage chunks linguica
linguica chunks of linguica Chomsky was grilling linguica
hosting a dinner party an informal dinner party at
his house his house on Cape Cod in Wellfleet Wellfleet
he was chomping on linguica Chomsky chomping
chomping Chomsky chomping linguica in his house

famous linguist and anarchist too
Israelphobic pious progressive Jew

Chomsky radically chomping off chomping off then spitting out
a burnt black chunk of linguica chomping off then spitting
out a flawed and repellant ideology ideology
a flawed and repellant ideology chomping linguica in his house

famous linguist and anarchist too
Israelphobic pious progressive Jew

Chomsky radically chomping off chomping off and spitting out
a burnt black chunk of linguica Chomsky grilling linguica
hosting a dinner party saying the pro-Israel Jewish lobby are
the bad Jews Chomsky sucking a Portuguese sausage chomping
linguica in his house

famous linguist and anarchist too
Israelphobic pious progressive Jew

hosting a dinner party an informal dinner party chomping
linguica at charming Chomsky house on Cape Cod in charming
colonial Wellfleet Chomsky radically chomping off chomping
off then spitting out a burnt black chunk of linguica
Chomsky radically chomping off chomping off then spitting out
a burnt black chunk of linguica chomping off then spitting
out a flawed and repellant ideology ideology of a

famous linguist and anarchist too
Israelphobic pious progressive Jew

Chomsky radically chomping off and spitting out a burnt black
chunk of linguica saying members of progressive movements
who happen to be Jewish are the good Jews ideology of a

famous linguist and anarchist too
Israelphobic pious progressive Jew

Chomsky radically chomping off a chunk of bloody ideology
grilling it well done burning all the blood away offering
the chunks to his cronies Zionism equals Nazism chomping down
hard a chunk of bloody ideology Israel an isolated pariah
linguistics linguica ideology smoked tongue enormous respect
of leftists for Chomsky tongue chomping down hard and chomping
off a bloody chunk of his tongue bloody chunk of Chomsky tongue
gossip and slander Israel an isolated pariah
Gossip and slander loshen hora
Gossip and slander loshen hora
a chunk of bloody ideology

famous linguist and anarchist too
Israelphobic pious progressive Jew

*

The voice the voice the voice
of the tapeworm the voice of an alien
in the house in the house in the house
of Noam Chomsky imitating imitating the flat line
the flat line monotone monotone
voice of Chomsky the breath of the tapeworm
blowing kisses blowing kisses along
the digestive tract of the linguist while
grilling chunks of linguica chomping linguica in his house

famous linguist and anarchist too
Israelphobic pious progressive Jew

Deceit prances in prances in prances into charming
Chomsky house the house that Chomsky built the charming
Chomsky house on ocean side Chomsky grilling linguica
grilling grilling globules of fat sizzling sizzling sizzling
spattering sputtering muttering
a secret tribal language chomping linguica in his house

famous linguist and anarchist too
Israelphobic pious progressive Jew

A secret tribal language muttering sputtering globules
fat spatterings fat and gristle sizzling sizzling
exposing a flawed and repellant ideology ideology
ideology of Chomsky's vanguard of judeophobia
passing gas squatting on his hobby horse
passing gas the breath of the tapeworm blowing kisses
belching platitudes to his cronies blowing kisses
along the digestive tract of the linguist
the tapeworm looping its segments
looping a noose of Jewish self-hatred an Uncle Noam
relaxing his sphincter his flat line monotone
again and again the voice of the tapeworm
the voice of an alien imitating the monotone monotone
voice of Chomsky grievous violations of bad Jews
of Israel vehemently deplored by the Wellfleet
Deplore Israel Organization who are of

double standard persuasion Intelligentsia
of Academia chomping linguica in his house

famous linguist and anarchist too
Israelphobic pious progressive Jew

Intelligentsia of Academia in their secret enclave
on Cape Cod in colonial Wellfleet Wellfleet
with beautiful New England architecture classical revival churches
where no blacks sing where the word 'WASP'
was invented by a wasp in the house in the house
in the house of Chomsky in Chomsky's house
the voice of the tapeworm the voice of an alien
imitating the monotone flat line goose-stepping
Chomsky voice goose-stepping in a vanguard
of Chomsky judeophobia the Chomsky tongue
coated with fat and gristle articulating tongue
of an ideologue living high on the linguica chomping Chomsky

famous linguist and anarchist too
Israelphobic pious progressive Jew

The tongue of the linguist swelling swelling swelling
ten times its size the tapeworm segmenting segmenting
the linguist articulating articulating a flawed
a flawed and repellant a flawed and repellant
ideology Zionism equals Nazism
the body of the tapeworm segmenting segmenting
generating generating its body a language chunks chunks
of itself folding into itself folding into itself into totem
and taboo into totem and taboo folding into itself
the breath of the tapeworm blowing kisses along
the digestive tract of the linguist the tapeworm
folding itself folding itself
into the totem-scrotum the totem-scrotum of a

famous linguist and anarchist too
Israelphobic pious progressive Jew

Again and again grilling grilling chunks of linguica
the taste buds of the tongue of the linguist
goose-stepping coated with peppery fat and gristle
the fat globules of the Protocols of Chomsky
in his secret enclave the house that Chomsky built
his cronies chomping Portuguese sausage grilling
Chomsky grilling the breath of the tapeworm blowing
kisses the pornographic vision of Otto Weininger
and judeophobic Jews Uncle Noams
the tapeworm segmenting segmenting segmenting
propagating propagating propagating
blowing kisses along the digestive tract
of Chomsky chomping linguica in his house

famous linguist and anarchist too
Israelphobic pious progressive Jew

*

In the floor of the mouth of the mouth of Chomsky
the linguist the moving organ articulates
the Chomsky tongue grilling grilling grilling
linguica articulating articulating articulating
a secret tribal language
in the house of Chomsky in the house
on ocean side on Cape Cod the Chomsky sphincter
tightening in the Führer-mouth the Führer-mouth
taste buds of Chomsky tongue germinating germinating
spores of pathological fury of a

famous linguist and anarchist too
Israelphobic pious progressive Jew

The moving organ swelling the organ in the floor
of the mouth of Chomsky the Führer of Judeophobes
the moving organ the tongue of Chomsky swelling
a hundred times its size craving licking burning chunks
rupturing flesh of arms legs brains blistering
black grapes blistering lungs kidneys liquifying

melting under a vanguard of Jew hatred
a black-belt of martyrdom of a homicide bomber
a black-belt of holiness a black-belt of dynamite
a black-belt of sacred text twisting into ideology
"Israel has no right to exist" a homicide bomber's vision
of purity rupturing flesh blistering black grapes
blistering under the white skull of the Jerusalem sun

*

In the house of Chomsky on ocean side on ocean side
in colonial Wellfleet Wellfleet on Cape Cod
in charming Chomsky house in the house of a princess
a cherished daughter of a

famous linguist and anarchist too
Israelphobic pious progressive Jew

In the house of Chomsky during summer nights
in charming Chomsky house the cicadas droning droning
during summer nights in colonial Wellfleet Wellfleet
cooling breezes blowing Cape Cod country curtains
blowing blowing lyrically in the cherished Chomsky
house cooling breezes blowing cooling all the bedrooms
breezes cooling all the bedrooms of the Chomsky
family home on ocean side on Cape Cod in colonial
Wellfleet Wellfleet pristine art galleries
classical revival churches where no blacks sing

In the house of an ideologue living high on the linguica
the huge bulk of the tongue of Chomsky
a maxi-publishing industry anarchism imperialism
the huge bulk of the tongue of the Mengele
of linguistics segmenting segmenting segmenting
goose-stepping goose-stepping goose-stepping
the Jewish Judeophobe the huge bulk of the tongue
of Chomsky the pornographic vision of Otto Weininger
Intelligentsia of Academia the huge bulk of the tongue
of Chomsky the huge bulk of Chomsky tongue a veritable

maxi-publishing industry anarchism imperialism
grilling grilling grilling linguica chomping chomping
chomping the huge bulk of the tongue of Chomsky
germinating guinea worms from out of the dark bulk
of the tongue of a

famous linguist and anarchist too
Israelphobic pious progressive Jew

Guinea worms streaming out of the taste buds
of Chomsky tongue the efficient Chomsky tongue
the dark bulk of the tongue of the linguist
segmenting pieces segmenting "Israel's intransigence
Israel a pariah" grilling grilling grilling
"Zionism equals Nazism" the sphincter tightening
tightening the lowest part of the Chomsky body
an ideologue living high on the linguica
the efficient Chomsky tongue pregnant with guinea worms
the dark bulk a masterpiece of capitalist enterprise
the huge bulk of the tongue of Chomsky set in the
lowest part the lowest part of the skull of Chomsky
the Chomsky jawbone the chosen jawbone the Chomsky jawbone
the chosen jawbone unhinging hinging unhinging hinging
the chosen jawbone of a

famous linguist and anarchist too
Israelphobic pious progressive Jew

Sacred Place

Drawing a straight line in the air
a baldheaded pilgrim
from Belgium
singing 'on the road again'
journeying to some sacred place
journeying to Santiago di Compostela
seeing dollars
drachmas euros francs liras
marks pesos pounds
renminibi shekels yen
singing 'on the road again'
journeying to some sacred place
journeying to Santiago di Compostella
hitting the thrift stores
estate sales flea markets
remembering a woman
smashing herbs
with the side of a knife
singing 'on the road again'
journeying to some sacred place
journeying to Santiago di Compostella
piled up sketches
the crucified one
the scourged martyrs
slapping flying insects
insects far and near
singing 'on the road again'
journeying to some sacred place
journeying to Santiago di Compostella
debeaked chickens in cages
the tracks of wild ducks
slapping flying insects
insects far and near
dollars euros pesos
drachmas francs liras marks pounds
renminbi shekels yen
a baldheaded pilgrim from Belgium

singing 'on the road again'
journeying to some sacred place
journeying to Santiago di Compostella
slapping flying insects
insects far and near
tracing his nerve endings
the roof of his skull
the shape of his brain
slapping flying insects insects far and near
like passionate lovers
thirsting for his sweat
dollars euros pesos
filling his money belt
sweet lucre under his heart
like an unborn babe
in its amniotic sac
a baldheaded pilgrim from Belgium
weeping praying
spiritual soul animal hole
spiritual hole animal soul
journeying to some sacred place
journeying to Santiago di Compostella
weeping praying
animal soul spiritual hole
animal hole spiritual soul
journeying to some sacred place

Woman of Jesus

It is about skin
and hair of the yoga mistress
from Rosario Portugal
remember how I said her hair
was a long hanging rope
winding down
her collarbone
under her armpits
hanging down
her breastbone
ravenous the skin pulling apart
the skin like
the petals of flowers
ravenous the knives of Portugal
repetitive rhythmical
monotonous hacking off bones
slicing off rotting flesh
remember how I said
the hard horny skin and hair
shedding dead cells
transforming becoming a bud
becoming a bud
a flower a pale green lily
emerging from the mud
a place where oysters breed
from the mud of Rosario Portugal
remember how I said

unearthly pale and red light

her skin and hair
remember how I said magnetic
metal striking clashing
her voice saying
"les Portugais sont de grand voyageurs"
remember how I said
she had washed the bodies

of amputees
winding the bandages
how she had clothed and fed
the maimed
of automobile accidents of train wrecks
of war
attaching their prosthetic limbs
humming and singing in Portuguese
seeing them come back to life
rising up like Lazarus
like Lazarus rising from the grave
her kindness banishing evil
from the world

unearthly pale and red light

remember how I said
she dreamed of a black bull
of Portugal
amputated at the knees
she dreamed of a laughing dwarf
with a virginal face

unearthly pale and red light

it is about how she stood before
a hive of bees listening—
Barbara De Jesus of Rosario Portugal

unearthly pale and red light
the yoga mistress breathing
the long rows of students breathing
bending their hands backwards
like Balinese dancers
skin and hair shedding dead cells
remember how I said
she sat on the heel of one foot
chanting chanting chanting
lingam yoni natal cleft vida morte

vida morte lingam yoni natal cleft
vida morte vida morte

unearthly pale and red light

Museum Curator in a Cube

for Braque and Picasso

Evoking the rhythm of
rhythm of spontaneous changes
the artifact from Africa

heating to the temperature
the temperature of human skin
the artifact from Africa

warming the arms back and chest
of the curator
the artifact from Africa

warming the shoulders and wrists
of the curator
the artifact from Africa

rays of light penetrating
the biceps flexing contracting
the artifact from Africa

resting on the palm
the palm of the curator
the artifact from Africa

smooth as the skin of an apple
glowing warmly
the artifact from Africa

in the palm of the hand
of the curator
the artifact from Africa

lying on the palm
the palm of the curator
the artifact from Africa

the hand of the curator
warming the wood
the artifact from Africa

the hand cupping the little god
the eyes seeing
the artifact from Africa

in the head of the curator
seeing the eyes opening
the artifact from Africa

the long neck
of the little god stretching
the artifact from Africa

the little god bending twisting
the biceps flexing contracting
the artifact from Africa

the rump hips and thighs
totem and taboo totem and taboo
the artifact from Africa

rays of light
illuminating the scrotum
the artifact from Africa

the feet circling
feet and toes jabbing
the artifact from Africa

toenails jabbing into the palm
of the curator
the artifact from Africa

the biceps flexing contracting
the rump hips and thighs
the artifact from Africa

rays of light penetrating
the feet and toes
the artifact from Africa

toenails jabbing forcing
deeper deeper into the palm
the artifact from Africa

blood pushing to the surface
oozing drops of blood
the artifact from Africa

pounding deeper deeper
the nails into the palm
the artifact from Africa

the iron nails a silence
in the palm of a hand
the artifact from Africa

in the head of the curator
the ears hearing
the artifact from Africa

breathing swallowing the breath
passing voiceless
the artifact from Africa

the arms and legs tapering
the breath of the little god
the artifact from Africa

the breath of the little god
inhaling exhaling
the artifact from Africa

the breath of the curator
inhaling exhaling
the artifact from Africa

the breath passing voiceless
voiceless as a fish
the artifact from Africa

voiceless as a fiery particle
voiceless as a bed of ashes
the artifact from Africa

glowlng warmly in the palm
the palm of the hand of the curator
the artifact from Africa

evoking the rhythm of
rhythm of spontaneous changes

Poeming the Bambino

Biting the apple
hungrily
the little wooden bambino
animates

his rosebud mouth an irregular shape

playing with blocks
the little wooden bambino
predicts
disease famine torture war

divination
a handful of earth flung down
beyond the edges
of a page

is a spider rendering light

texture and surface
an irregular shape
neither floral foliation
nor avian undulates

identity unknown

writing on the wall
the 24th letter of the alphabet
Xenophon and Xerxes

like a rapid chemical change
the deed neither good nor evil

a viper searching
a viper flinging itself searching
its barbed tail an innovation

the circumstance orbiting
orbiting the sun
like a whirling dervish

the little wooden bambino
an apple and a knife

paring the apple
without breaking the peel
spoiling three apples

throwing the parings
the letter X

the farmer's wife
with a carving knife

in a bucolic setting
a philosopher begins devouring
a light meal sweet cakes
sake and thick tea

in her gut
a rapid chemical change
in a fat fold of her abdomen
sacred writ

in a fold of rock strata
destruction

the weight of the viper a thought

*

The little wooden bambino
thinking—once upon a time

the little wooden bambino
holding a hot wire
cutting out letters

c o v e t o u s

naming letters counting letters

a p p l e

his rosebud mouth an irregular shape
covetous brotherly love

velvety jet black his eyes

counting his wooden fingers
playing with letters
s p e l l i n g

disease famine torture war

the little wooden bambino
chanting—
"in my father's house"

on the stone floor
an unknown word

an apple tree growing
beyond the edges of a page

under the apple tree
dead and putrefying

a word neither good nor evil

the little wooden bambino
holding a hot wire
cutting out letters

bright colors the letters
letters of black fire

luminous the eyes eyes
of the little wooden bambino
his rosebud mouth an irregular shape

an apple tree growing
limbs and leaves undulating
beyond the edges of a page

*

Amazed at the sound
the little wooden bambino
l i s t e n s

the blocks falling
on a stone floor
"in my father's house"

Amazed at the touch
The little wooden bambino
f e e l s

an icon hanging
on a nail
"in my mother's house"

Amazed at the sight
the little wooden bambino
s t a r e s

on my mother's face
a melancholy look

disease famine torture war

a spider rendering light

on my mother's face
one eye cut into pieces

covetous brotherly love

Amazed at the smell
the little wooden bambino
i n h a l e s

poison

an apple and a knife
paring the apple
without breaking the peel

throwing the parings
beyond the edges
of a page

disease famine torture war

Amazed at the taste
the little wooden bambino
b i t e s

an apple

his rosebud mouth an irregular shape

covetous brotherly love
beyond the edges of a page

Color Pool in Umbria

In memoriam Al Held

First a question
then an outline
is it an anatomical form

the monumental painting
is it bearing a signature
and are the letters blurred?

Again the question
the monumental painting
is it an anatomical form

a form of optical effects
of peculiar power
is it bearing a signature

and are the letters blurred?

*

A dead man in a pool
closely and intimately the smell
of chlorine

dead in the swimming pool
of his Umbrian Villa
gorgeous the stone work

painted tiles medieval ruins
the drowned artist's passion
his rural Eden

monumental the golden mosaic
the giant Cyclops
the gleaming brutal eye

splintering sunlight grapevines
fields of sunflowers olive groves
the drowned artist floating
circling drifting round and round
his rural Eden
a color pool of aquamarine

a dead man's float
the full sweet lips open

Incredible the beauty
of the Umbrian maid a girl of fifteen
a farmer's daughter

the muscles of her back
spirally arranged her honey-tone hands
slipping under layers of water

the drowned artist floating beyond
further and further
moving in circles diagonals

ovals rectangles squares
moving beyond the honey-tone hands
further and further
the drowned artist seized

seized by Cyclops the giant
jittery energy the body of work
is work of the body

drifting geometries

*

Incredible the beauty
of the Umbrian maid a girl of fifteen
on her knees

moving in circles
polishing the marble floor
a farmer's daughter

singing 'amore mio amore mio'
the marble floor sparkling
smiling at her reflection

the full sweet lips open
In the afternoon
sipping Umbrian wine

tearing off the wing of
a roast pigeon a breast vein
as thick as a finger

*

Everyday Disturbances
in Umbrian farm country

sipping white wine
the faythful cut their tongues out

it is possible that a discarded wallet
holds the beggar spellbound

overzealous crushing the grapes
dangerous and violent the fruit

when the fish gasped Jesus laughed
the full sweet lips open

pulling off the skin of the fish
like a glove hearing a mourning dove

succulent the fillet rolled
rapturous the tongue of the monk

the volume of the fish sea water
spilled on the putrefied heart

Elegy of a Convict

The old convict seeing
a photo an antler of a stag

seeing the horns of a bull
fragile the bones

the bones of a bull rider
yellow the bones

white the summer blossoms
a girl in his arms

her hips swaying
white her summer dress floating

her hips swaying
between her thighs the black rose
between his eyes a shrunken head
a knife in a loaf of bread

white her summer dress floating
an old tattoo on withered skin

the word 'captivity'
O Mistress Mine My Lady

My Lady growing
out of a mound of dirt

My Lady growing out of rotten meat
out from core and root

out of an ant hill a waft of air
her apple scented skin

my toothless mouth gentle its kiss
my wounded woman

her apple scented skin
My Queen of Hearts My Marilyn

The old convict whispering—
my ulcerous tongue

broken your knuckles
ripped the callus of your foot

The old convict washing her feet
torn your ligaments

your coffee brown nipples
erect like my thumbs

The old convict trembling
I'm under your thumb

passionate my gums
my toothless mouth gentle its kiss
The old convict digging
small holes from front to back

from back to front
seeing endless endless summer blossoms

crouching over the earth
white the summer blossoms swaying

squatting over the earth
her hips swaying between her thighs

the black rose
an old tattoo on withered skin

The old convict hearing
a singing cowboy—mine is the power

The old convict digging small holes
putting in the ground
the root of love
My Queen of Hearts My Marilyn

folding in the ground
words words of velvety fur

words about to make a kill
My Queen of Hearts My Marilyn

words of small eyes
words of fossorial forefeet

My Queen of Hearts My Marilyn

Never Having Seen a Wave

for Stavros Deligiorgis

Never having seen a wave
frozen in mid-air the glassblower

manifold images in his brain
the rays of the sun

amorphous the forms boiling forming
a floating toothed leaved plant

floating Acanthus
a Black Hole a crucible a bubble glowing

one millionth one millionth of a second
an episode

a ferocious s c a t t e r i n g
white ovals glassy crystals orbiting
never having seen a wave
frozen in mid-air the glassblower

turning spinning blowing hail-stones
shaping winds oceans storms

storms eddying
layers of ice cracking piling lifting

molten glass swelling lifting arching
never having seen a wave

frozen in mid-air the glassblower
dipping into the furnace

around and around rolling and shaping
around and around

a gob of molten glass
melting shards spiraling flaring
glittering hot glass
amorphous dazzling light frozen

in the glassblower's brain
hot glass spiraling around and around

amorphous the glass
never having seen a wave frozen in mid-air

cooling scattering flowing
s u s p e n d e d

molten the ice the winds circling
a billion suns

the breath of the glassblower
the brain of the glassblower

moisture and nutrients flowing
the glassblower's skull
the skull the color of snow
ferocious the heat pouring melting

melting and freezing the seas
spiraling arms

out of the crucible the glassblower
gathering gathering

never having seen a wave frozen in mid-air
rolling lifting arching

the layers of glass surging surging

The Fabulist

On the pale yellow wall
above the frame an apparition

piles of rocks the nomad's camp
the village on fire

an unlit cigar in the fabulist's mouth
the still wet brownish color

a smell of autumnal decay

In the galleries of Japanese Art
ambling meandering strolling

zigzagging zipping past
heads shoulders hands hips feet

rushing through unpainted space
a photo of a mushroom cloud
an asymmetrical form

an unlit cigar in the fabulist's mouth
the still wet brownish color

a smell of autumnal decay

In the galleries of Romantic Art
joining the wedding feast

a tribal elder chewing hashish
a little boy eating a nut cake

a skeletal frame
the limbs spreading apart

cinnamon cumin and honey
savory the smoke of roasting meat

the clerk who is a fabulist
who calls herself Ezra

Ezra kicking the goat head
a goat smile on her lips

slender and elongated is Ezra
swaying from side to side

from her pocket springs a flower
out of the hole of Baudelaire

vomiting the bride and groom
long ago an hour ago

only a minute
strolling through unpainted space

a photo of a mushroom cloud
an asymmetrical form
autumnal ivy leaves
beginning above the frame

heads shoulders hands hips feet
piles of rocks the nomad's camp

the village on fire
an unlit cigar in the fabulist's mouth

the still wet brownish color
a smell of autumnal decay

The Tree Cutter

At dawn the tree cutter
under an occult sky

of greens and yellows
climbing higher and higher

considers the trades
of butchers dyers sailors

considers the calling
of artists dancers musicians

the tree cutter hearing the blues
the blues of B. B. King

climbing higher and higher
into wilderness

a nomad and a wanderer
a wanderer in a strange land

seeing organic forms forms
of stems roots a donkey's tail

the faces of mummies
the curves of hardened sap

cutting into bark
the tree cutter seeing mobiles

geometric shapes houses
of the Cyclades the Bauhaus

changing shifting circles
a frenzy of wood chips a spastic dance

a spastic dance of wood chips
witnessed by grackles
the tree cutter hearing
staccato notes lopping off twigs

cutting away diseased parts
raised bumps bulbous deformity

into a vertical wilderness
climbing higher and higher

cutting cutting cutting
working working the tree cutter

contemplating Particle Theory
resting in the crotch of the tree

in the tree cutter's brain
the flow of hormonal forces

in the trunk of the tree
a flow of moisture and nutrients
an unearthly glow
like the effects of the moon

sitting cross-legged
in the crotch of the tree

meditating on the cutting
the selected branches

musing on the languid tendrils
of pubic hair

sorcery of his female brain
climbing higher and higher

a wilderness of curving rhythmic
forms twisting reptilian

rotting snakelike branches
chopping away the branches
emerald the leaves whirling
whirling above

redundant the leafless branches
useless the branches

the tree cutter hearing
a Bach Cantata

contemplating Particle Theory
a flush of wet hot air

burning his neck and face
the flow of hormonal forces

feeling a twisting a binding
a corset of pain binding

the pain a passage
glorious the pain binding

from

Not Be Essence That Cannot Be

(1961)

(Bom) Only Checkerberry

(Pukist)
    Behold!
        (Winter)
        (Winter)
Ned.
Dog. Nigra. Boodle
Dulia. Pungent. Pelidna dum
Dum. Work
Mediterranean
Mediterranean
Gloominess
(Pagouros)
Crasy Shakespeares
Midsummer
Jynx
Past and wrong
(Bom) only checkerberry
Yields shits (cucumis)
            (Winter)
             (Winter)
Spicy red berries (winter)
                (winter)
Wart hog joy.

Say Old English Wishe Me

th th
twease my paws My voice her tits
was loafs of bread just dadabeeyah
sap south-pole jipa savejoy
three bladders say old english
wishe me
sweet-loss
suck lent drool
infallible
meat broke
scab lip lips whistling
with the nose
beget rejib   horrible in th
th th
pencil wish me twitch
sea raven
just
dadabeeyah

Ma Nip (Go Away)

my bullet ma be a good gel
    MA KISS FLAGRANTLY
Ma nip (go away) slightly
nebuLOUSEly miMICKing
like a shadow (butcher)
coMINGing on Shekinah
carving the Slovaks man nananimal
man nananimal
    Slaz the harvest fly's
hard meat HARD 'nd harmless
ma I'm natural (but)
Ma nip (go away) slightly

Zu Zu Midday I'm Narcotic

Endlong skirmish lump
I am gallant, greek
Nightingale, zu zu
Midday I'm narcotic,
Light, ball-flowered
Fly, ku ku ven-omous
Beyond wood luring
Stick, polled, over

My mucous, meaning
Many me's hot-short
Poor snakemouth I
Sence eels sneering
My forward voo doo
To and fro, seven
puffs, to and fro
ME, white-colored

YOU muck luck dope
A evil drink, top
Of a wapiti poyo,
YOU goo me bloodshot
YOU whacky fop, O Oph
Elia you milk the
Pocket-knife poko
On holidays in the sun

I'll Still Have

                    be jeered at
              spot brown
       on me
    & harass
                          i'm putrid
                    i'm lowest
                    (i suffer meanly)
       of them with the symbol
                alway
          & my nose is inflamed
                                  roasted meat
              lap the drippings
                (i should not)
have the   brown
                    on me
                       O openly
              nocuous
       not ever kiss
            & give up
                    buzzing away
       (speaking distinctly)
              to the bare ear
          (O my long tail)
                                      i'll still
have   i'll have
              Nizam
    & jaw & nose
            my gut wall
one foot long

Dripping Thing Four Legs

Till she's dead, cult-
Ivated (zool zool) lady's
Finger upon her, waiting
Forming sweet bacteria
Dripping Thing Four
Legs between Needed
Four legs Great Maria

Insanity. And the alco-
Holic Not satiable high
Ner-vous hindiihideous
Cr-ime, exaggerated.
Woman. In ripening no
Accomplishment Head with-
Out Urine Harsh absol-

Ute. Yupun cedar Crotch.
Of a human being Actively
Cool. Risen piggishly Conk-
Ed Supported jeered, involv-
Ing knotgrass branches as
Come out two serpents kill-
Ing. With pipes. Pink and

Stinking Forth. Below. Mam-
Mals Either lick of a group
Side of bad female propagated
With a war-m day of spring Afri-
Cans unfeeling-ly think of fo-
Od Meat dried hard. Eat-en
By men and women Hook the shank.

AB Branches of Trees

Udo Udo sto-
Ut, wilted
Vital snot
(In the urine, eyelashes)
(In the sack, big monoto-
Nous snot, again)

Unsegmented, we croak
Wax cylinder to remember
Us by Hebdomadal fuck you
Lame as a game dog
(In a woman's shape)
(Contains eternal tick fever
Thuja. Bear it)

Croak you ag-
Ain seasons, ab bran-
Ches of trees, noose
Fastened, unkempt
Swinging (In a organism, gray white
Goose-fit)

Hera Hera Hera

You Ye; The bee's jail, Puck workhouse
YOU YE zealous spongy devoting to
Fucking logic, bath-ing in the
Stream, giggling. Laying pros
Titutes lowly, Mary Eddy
Lengthwise, Mahatma the beholder,
Relieving trickiness above one leap year
Eating cucumber. Opposed to the crotch crotch
Hucking honeybee
Boiling the ruuts
The hognut lower down mewing
Screwing, The giant ragweed,
And feeling the loneliness
Staining
Yellow green.
Crookneck with bark whorish
Europe bones divide
Mad shame and kissing
Sweetmeats. My lord very good
In the mind
You Ye whose
Crack open
After after after sap drain, stealth, Hera Hera
Hera

O Wafersh Tashte Good

o 6) o glutinous
o glot of glory
do an earthquake
o shockhead (50ft)
piss backward b
o special friend
twice o chrissakes,
b o natural man
(again in confession o wafersh tashte good)
shlike new, sho pleashe!
fixsh my marriagesh
everyshling allright
shknock shknock help!
shling shling
a brigadier shcould
it, itsh sho bad
o engineershz fixsh
(fluk hurricane was bad weather shtoilet shlike)
it itsh shzown shthe
MY FLUSH, stush
hung mush (Mrs) agony
cooed o bridesmad
crosh a fem and o
monthly maN is bad
o thief o shush
(Mrs) agony hung
(an animal pick worthy pick jist in jail breath)
out skullcap breed
o agony cooed
(Mrs)

from

Salt & Core

(1968)

Old Waiter

old grandfather
they'll waylay
you take you
by the ribs
& make you
carry dishes
they'll force
you to breathe
in steam your
toes will
turn inward
(your unhealthy
tissues like
a poor bird)
you'll have
to kiss hands
like a german
a white taste
will be in
your mouth horr-
ible & stick
in your clothing
it itches your
bulgarian name
will make them
smile
"who, what?", you'll
say your ear like
a preserved meat
won't hear well

Concertina Song

in a hen-
house maybe
in 1133 at
the foot of
it was some
kind of fruit
fruit-eating
things
in 1133
at the foot
in a whore-
house maybe
in 1133
at the foot
of it was
some narrow
minded bastards
who wanted the
place closed
then shyest
people could
not even look
at the foot
without think-
ing of pubic
hairs in a hen-
house maybe
in 1133

I Am Very Excited, It's July the 3rd and I Am on a Destroyer

I am dressed perfectly for my venture
                                        with sailors
        my hair is dark copper
        it hides my skull
        which shields the pulpy orange
                of my brain; my brain is fruit
    I am in black bell-bottoms
I am dressed perfectly for my venture
                                    with sailors

        I am aboard—I ask George not
    to kill my joy—he lets me alone
        & I walk very lithe with golden hoops
                    in my ear lobes
            & sailors watch me like scared children
                sailors smile to me like friendly
        sisters
                sailors wait for me to possess
            them!
                            I ask one how old the Destroyer
                        is, a little fellow whose eyes
                                    reach my throat
                        "20 years old, Maam",
    he is wistful as I lope away
                        towards a cluster of sailors
                            all looking at my hair
                                    eyes
                                        bell-bottoms
                            & breasts
I notice that some of the sailors look
                        like chubby women with good hearts
                            they are easy to smile at—
        but sticking to the rules of my game
            with a quivering drawn dagger in my smile
                    I look at a beautiful cruel one
                            he just stares at me like

a coat checking attendant
who I do not tip—
for some reason he would
not smile
'to hell with you', I think.
—then I see at the front end
of the ship a chubby dark pirate smiling sweetly
& I smile sweetly back as I approach
we chat about the sun
& his tattoo
—a cluster of sailors is watching us
& one with his arm in a sling, his pretty middy
torn up the waist, comes to the
pirate & I
he is blond & wears glasses
I think 'a sailor should not wear glasses'
& I do not like his teeth
but he has a tattoo
& he says the right things
—how a sailor gets drunk every
two days, etc.
I take the cigarette the
pirate offers me
the sun is too hot
I am bored
I go away smiling
—I happen to look down the opening
to the bottom of the Destroyer
& a handsome sailor joyfully
waves to me, he acts as if
he wants me to climb
down
I don't
bye bye I wave
bye bye destroyer

Let Us Honor Them, the Clichés Which Have Got Us All by the Throat

I like
dead residue (a good phrase)
it is not very cliché
but
THE DARK RECESSES OF THE HUMAN MIND,
that is very cliché
the clichés are fantastically
true, like
POUND IS A GREAT POET
THO' HE IS A FASCIST
Hold! Wait!
POUND IS A GREAT POET
THO' HE *WAS* A FASCIST
the old man had a
CHANGE OF HEART
ha ha
(note *change of heart*)
a big cliché
but back to THE DARK RECESSES OF THE HUMAN MIND
it can be altered to
THE SHADOWY CREVICES OF THE HUMAN MIND
(tho' that sounds sexual, shadowy crevices)
HE PRESSED HIS FACE AGAINST HER SHADOWY CREVICES
SHADOWY CAVERNS!
that's better!
THE SHADOWY CAVERNS OF THE HUMAN MIND!
"TO CLOUD MENS MINDS"
& womens too
(that's very familiar)
WHEREBY THEY ARE CONFUSED!
ha ha a
CONFUSION OF TONGUES
Babel?
delightful?
A confusion of tongues licking
us all over

ha ha

Now that is not a cliché
neither is a polyglot of tongues
licking us all over
only a fine poet
would use
polyglot of tongues
only a poet with
an ear of excellence
would think up
a polyglot of tongues
licking
us all over

For, Behold The Day Cometh, That
Shall Burn As An Oven; And All The
Proud, Yeah, And All That Do Wickedly,
Shall Be Stubble: And The Day That
Cometh Shall Burn Them Up, Saith The
Lord Of Hosts, That It Shall Leave Them
Neither Root Nor Branch, Yeah.

for the pentagon

Why call an anti-missile
Nike-Zeus
why not Flaming-Jesus
or Red-Eye Moses
We are a Judeo-Christian
cIvIlIzAtIoN
are we not?
why the hang-up
on ancient Hellenic
Gods!
What is it with
us!

What's wrong with calling
a bomb
St. Mary or
Big-Joel
what's wrong with
Jewish names
or Christian ones!
Are the weapons so brilliant & ruddy
like cocks
so virile
in the eyes of the Pentagon
that they must
be given
the names of pagan gods!
Why not Baal!
that's a good name

or St. Luke!
                    aren't they romantic enough!
Why Nike-Zeus
                         why not Psalms or
                                                   Lamentations!

For Deacon Kevin

& you've given up
meat for lent,
father?
& you're arguing
with me
'bout
how you
are a pacifist
& the transfiguration
o' jesus
& I squint at you
for a ½ minute
& watch your
exquisite hands
flutter over
(breasts) a glass
of russian vodka
You will not touch pizza pie
nor meat nor chicken
nor woman
& I
look
at you & say
your way is fierce purity!
& I know you
like those sounds
& so
I
wet
my mouth
& call you a carnivore
hanging from a tree
& a sensualist
& you (23) agree
...billy-goat-faced-boy is your lover
across the table
& I had thought

of you reading books
& praying (only)
& so I think
it's your bag
& FATHER FATHER WHY HAST THOU...
O never mind

Between the Karim Shahir

man-apes
not at Steinheim!
but he doesn't hang
in Limbo—
the face is pretty
brutish
put together from
a sack of old bones
their heads were neither
low or primitive
spearheads stone picks
stone teeth & chopping
tools—
rivers yield water-logged
wooden idols,
everybody was so
advanced
over the europe of
8000 years
great joy!
suddenness
no longer living like
animals
(O those lucky food producers)
their specialty:
horse, dog
pregnant woman
worship the watermelon
venus—
found pigs
in the latest levels
(O those nile udders
give my lips a rash)
We know they had goats & sheep
porridge bowls
parch it—
crack it, reap grain, wheat

& eat up
So the Jarmo people
grew barley
2 different kinds
of wheat &
grew a barley plant
there's not a too clear picture
between the Karim Shahir
M'lefaat-Zawi
record says
in the
Kurdish hills

from

I Am the Babe of Joseph Stalin's Daughter

(1972)

Muddy Waters & the Whirlwind

for Dr. Tannenbaum

muddy waters was sing
ing
muddy waters & I
didn't even know
(I stood before
Baal & I knew that
Yahveh would hear me)
.it was muddy waters
how many drachmas is it
for a warm wood bowl
of the beloved's blood
in sweet   holy
JERUSALEM
Nobody ever caused me to be carried away captive/
I ran.
Like a gay prancing
golden hind/
muddy waters eats & drinks every
boundless creation day
of
exquisite song!

All I want you to know is: GREAT IS MY MERCY
but
great also/
is
my
CHASTISEMENT!
sing i sing i. & king
mud
dy

Baal drinks
50 gallons of wine
& stops all REVOLUTION AGAINST HIM

he has his foes
all beaten
back/ THE KING HAS BECOME A JEW!
I saw the footprints of those who exude
TREASON from every mother's son's 7 sacred
open
i
ngs!
Till the ends of the earth I will defeat
their wickedness. And so when muddy waters
came up out of egypt
He sang out of the whirlwind!

Evolution

I

coon explains it
that we stood
erect
slowly
s
l
o
w
I
y
somebody was
the size of
a big gorilla
teeth looking
like man's
more
than the
chinese apes
what's your skull capacity
o coon
larger than a white-handed
gibbon?
i should
hope so

II

assistant leakey lay next to
Von Koenigs
wald
what a link
like Zeuner he
found his

findings
look ma i'm a caucasoid
see by my teeth?

o islands of indonesia
sweet pithecanthropus o
little infant skull
o homo mother-fucker
everybody
had to
originate somewhere
out of the hearts
of water
no. 100 was killed
somebody dropped a stone
what hell happened
at formosa that day
o the head-crushing o the
crushed skulls
o junius bird
who excavated

Song of Meat, Madness & Travel

I

dried meat
O glorious is dried meat.
my wife's breast in my hand
we stare at dried meat
is it not strange?

II

I pity her
now I pity her   the woman the woman
who calls
in a voice of white madness
Let me fetch you, let me fetch you!

III

I desired to go north
as a great singer and dancer
my ears my ears
there is singing in them
The big caribou cows and the big bulls
and men
watch for me

Medieval Christ Speaks on a Spanish Sculpture of Himself

honey & water
father & son
so am i
so chiefly
good
i would seem by virtu
two christs (2)
with butterbrown
hair & blessed
(2) yellow eyes
god himself
sees me faire
geometricians
crawl at my feet
my divinity
my highest blessedness!

mother mary kissed my carcass
thinketh she of me
on my holiness
my uncorruption
And everlastingness
i marvel even too
at gods knowledge simple
(2) fyry angels
sweet policemen
press their bosoms
on my knees
(base poets say i
received holy
erection)
like lusty puella
with impious thighs
wet eyes
earthly sighs
o

Exit from the Forbidden Land of the Butch Dyke

Diane,
I intend to
let you go I do not require
thee any longer   your softness
bugs me and I
want to break
off the affair   notice
my girl
I didn't say
awful affair   I might have
called it awful
but you & I
know dear sweet
soft girl that
our flesh making delicious papaya
kisses were singingly dreamingly
paradisially flowingly lightful
& delightful &
now my girl I pick up my pants!
I deftly snappily buckle my
belt & leave you
calling & crying after
me.
A woman leaves
a woman crying on the floor.
Ah girl,
but you brought out
the boy in me. & now I play
the rakish serious mouthed
grim-eyed man who somehow was not
ever near the
sterling white heart
of happyness when he
I & me lay next to thee.

Ah Diane, can a girl be a boy?
Can Iris, the Rhine daughters

& the rose of Sharon all blip & wink
at me can girl sing to girl in
boyish doggy yelping sounds?
Girl, I have a book to write & a tree
to plant or chop
a house to build
politics to create   girl, I have no need
any longer for your breasts, belly &
pot o'honey.
I make the grand exit from
the forbidden and strangely
marvelous
land of the butch
dyke.
I go with my guns
drawn
& a Gary Cooper
smile on
my lips
If ever I or my horse
happen to meet
an extra rich flesh cantalope
on the road.
I and my horse will
ponder on the bounty of God's
goodness & I will think
of your womb
& a Gary Cooper
smile again
will
shape
my mouth.
ciao. chick. ciao!

Wild Woman's Resentment of Fakery

You lousy bitch
you have insulted me
with my own grim
mythology
I guess this is
in the american scheme
of things, my betrayal.
My dear, I had visual-
ized you with perfect
woman's breasts breasts
of a damsel from the
northern renaissance
your legs pressed
together & wearing close-fitting
animal skins, wild smell
coming from your hands BIG as a drunken
demon, a funny thought is playing
about your fatal lips.
I notice something
ludicrous it makes
me dizzy what I notice
it doesn't fit in with
the picture I feel
nauseous

I force you up against
the 15th century tapestry like
an American Indian. I'm hopping on a
leg as I wind & hook a skein of your perfectly
infuriating blonde hair around my fists
pulling with my mighty strength!

I believed you to be
naturally blonde
but you you
dye your hair!
I am at the height of passionate conviction

as I kill you.
I am a humorless bridegroom,
a mad-dog perfectionist.

The Sky-Splitting Pink Rubber Bistro

One wants to be sitting in
maybe in Vienna I want
to be in Vienna in
a bistro
made of sky-splitting
pink rubber
when she walks in
I appear (formerly Henry
Miller)
now I'm a flickering
spyder-eyed
bottle-shaped breasted
portable electric-
lighted gunpowdered
hearted
beauty!
I'm a burst-of-light-woman
Wow!
Her teeth
clamp into my neck I see her round
persian melon dusky
hips f l o a t i n g past
my eyes
like hot red letters spelling
scudda hoo scudda hay
what a beautiful woman
to buckle my knees for
to forever
trail after
I am Henry
Miller turned,
ReInCaRnAtEd into a
beautiful girl!

I read Sanscrit on
her tit & function
as the U.S. government

all encompassing like the chinese wall
I hold the girl
& fence her in
to my golden fruit heart
we speak Viennese
together & eat little
cakes
she says I should be
Poet Laureate
of Vienna China!
& I should teach the love of magic
& girls
in a bistro
made of sky-splitting
pink rubber!

Lesson in Songmaking, Song of Kim

I

i live in Yorkville
i love Kim Novak. she says
the things that touch
just right.   she & I should
set up house-keeping
together.
At night we finger
the keys
a long time
before we go in
& make love.
We both think the same & she enjoys me,
my name, the way I look
in my raincoat.
My trenchcoat. When I turn my back
the back of my head says the Jews cause unemployment.

Kim Novak
agrees that pastry
is so good
hot cup of tea & Slovak
bourbon to wash
the threats
down.

Hail Mary Full Of Grace Why Hide Thy Tender
Fragile Face!

II

I would go
down
on Hong Kong
to swing my ass
near Kims.
I stand in an elevator my mother is sleeping
& doesn't know that I'm going up
to the 9th floor
to see Kim
Novak.
Every time she sees me she says, 'over here, Paul'
I look at her & say
you win, Kim.
She makes little
sexy sounds & we promise to use our heads
every second.
Tonight we're going
to kill some guy named Harry & steal
the
money.
Kim says, 'the loot'
She wears the highest heels & is so
blonde
I hope she doesn't
break
my
heart.
Tonight I waited for her
so
long.

Wistful Butch Poem

I would be wearing
a white on white hard
clean man's shirt
I would be ass bare
in slightly hot herring
bone pair of pants
I'd
have a black
Valentino
slipping
toupee
I'd wear this
magnificent
dress
as I knelt
between
your feet
kissing
the
earth!
I'd be given
a gorgeous medal
of honor
for looking so
good/
for becoming a
lover/
and yr
friend.
period

I Am the Babe of Joseph Stalin's Daughter

i watch Tai Chi per
forating my mind
Tai Chi!
exquisite waves
of body moving in 4
holy directions
it is sacred quiet
motion.
& then cracking open
my eyes, banging in like a fat
shoe, is an image of Joseph
Stalin's huge occidental
daughter Svetlana! she has given me
birth!   I swam out
of her fresh salty womb
the whites of my eyes
tinged pink from her blood—for I
had stared wide with blasting
eyes open! open as I
journeyed out   as I
sailed away
from the energy machine
of Stalin's daughter
I am saturated with her central Asian
aroma
my mother my mother
a ponderous dancing angel
who is
seed bearing &
satisfies me with her 30
fingers & toes & big brown nipples!
her brain
is a glittering storm cloud hanging
over Washington D. C.
she learns the language of America
& puts her boots on

sitting by the edge of
BLACK LAKE, her warm
arms coil around harps &
she croons me a lullaby
about higher physics & horny sixty year old
men who slip between her
teeth like
kingly copper chinese noodles
waving in Tai Chi
Tai Chi peacebiting
song!

Song of the Black Domestic

I

attica
scattica
breaks
your
bones. nixon looks over
u.a.r.
you pour
deadly
gasoline
over
his
fish sandwich
you wipe
his lips up with NOBLE
dirty
mop!
wap wap
Then you insult the boss lady
she dumb/white/scared
when you wash
filthy sink/basin
with your po'
hard Dominican brown
hand
you make the white woman
feel funny as you scrub
out sink
with the flat
of your
rough palm/
she get upset
when she see the sweat on
your face
O STOP
she say

II

Paul Blackburn's dead

my eyes
are red
from
crying
attica scattica
the hurricane's
over new york
the Cape
is

so
gloomy

the sunset drops
a weak sweet
hand
over
the black criminals
of
attica
scattica
pack
the rats up
drink
the last drop
of
pain!

III

what are the changes
in christ's
corpse?
dreamy bruised
eyes
stuck up behind the lid?
a kiss(er)
that only
a jewish mother
could love
my son the
dead ass

eating up my good son's
scholarships?
my other
son went to
Nebraska
& married an asthmatic
gentile
she twirled her pubic hair
with a poetic
finger

she was a dead (ringer)
for Marilyn Monroe
I think she sighed

a lot when the moon was VERY ROUND

What a zoologist
I'll make
when I grow
old
I'll study the routes of sandpipers & watch sand

rats

eat up the fat
pumpkins of
October!

IV

i'll k
n
o
c
k
you & bash you in the mouf
you go down like d
e
a
d ole man in the river
my daughter is still in the
homeland the
Dominican Republique
she put blue earrings in her
hands she
carry them out of the rich woman's house
she
never scrub toilets not
her eighteen years life
she so sweet her behind
like
a little angel
she smell behind her
knees like
cooking rice
she hate the
white rich kings of Spain/America
she want to
go & marry
a rich Cuban
with long finger/
nayl

and put a grass stalk
between her teeth
&
whistle
for time when she
having
a small one
to dress up like
the christ/CHILD
He follow Fidel
Castro & become
a good KiNg!
I laugh
& whisper in Church

Deebler Woman on the Avenue

I

it's always there.
lunch.
For free I see banana
& cocoanut.   Sometimes I run fast-
er than a dog
after lunch.

I go into the white woman's shops
I see yellow soap
shaped like a small
baby's hand
it smell
good.
Like meat w/
cream gravy
Christ's impressive finger pointing
at
my
fate.

II

for $3.00
I get my hair done shiny &
fan
c
y I eat a lt brown frank-
furter
& wonder about my
child with
the
broken back
in the Republique

nobody ever iducated my thoughts inside my head
I never know what
to write in poems
I never knew
about Odysseus
or Penelope
or Hektor
I never went to school
all I wanted was
a bright violet-
colored nylon scarf
to dazzle the Jewish furniture man
with so
he could give me
a
good
buy.

III

sometimes I see a 15 year old
man on the bus.
He look like my husband
the one who thought he had two banging dongs

bells
that went thru the day-lite
around the earth crumbled like bread

stars in the sky.

He is my bride-groom
with a coke
bottle in the hand
he give me sweet river to kiss from his

glass-ass
his peck-
er
blacker
than the
Brazil
sun.

IV

Yes-ter-day I
Deebler woman, Victoria stole
a man's job.
I thought I could
work it better the ener-gy
the water
in the veins
the fume
of my breath
stronger
&
more sacred than
His.

He was moving a clothes rack
of yellow waitress uniforms on the
avenue
5th avenue
he should have been on
the 7th
avenue
not the 5th the 5th
is
for parades
& the smiling children

they eat pop-

corn
& the inside of the
thighs is smoo-
th

& smelling a little of
dirty-ness.
I would take the
small ones
to
church
sunday after the monday.

V

When Deebler woman
was fifteen she learnt
to suck up
coffee like
an animal.
coffee she lapped
up like a dog
from the dish
held between her two black fingers.
not because
she was an animal or
didn't know
better but because
it cooled
(sharp hot coffee)
cooled quicker
so then she
would finish the coffee
much quicker
it would be cool
so very quick
she'd lap up

the warm coffee
with a little milk
& 3 spoons of sugar
it was
her break-
fast & faster than a
crazy dog she'd run after
drinking lapping
up the coffee so
quickly
the dirt of the rich white woman's house.

DEATH TO THOSE WHO MAKE
PEOPLE DRINK COFFEE LIKE
ANIMALS!

Deebler Woman in the Rose Garden

I'm a chinese foot
all silken & pointed!
I exist i'm baptised   i find a
delicatessen
i want something soft
to press down
i don't want to
buy anything i want
it just given!
Banana pulp hangs from jesus'
fingers he'
s
been eating
up whole pies that
mary leaves on the window-ledges.
do you think my english
is getting better?
i go to school now.

from

The Joe 82 Creation Poems

(1974)

I
The First Footsong of Wild-Man

self-knowledge
naturally
is to put a sword
in the
middle of yr heart

I am not a prophet! & I
like the German

students very much
They are terrific

says wild-man
O give me a new good mechanical gadget
so that I can plunge it

in yr ViOlEnT heart!

O sing Hanoi Haiphong!
LonDon
town.
Frank
furt
the Bells of St.
Harry
chime!

like it   or not
I possess a dangerous weapon / footsong!

sings wild-man

II
The Virgin's Baby Howling Boy Is Wild-Man's Christmas Song

POeM
PoEm
one a day
make the wild man run away

swing the iron
chain
brake-a-back

virtuous sent-
iment
crack yr neck!

sing christmas peep!
bird-song foot / song christian snot
rots o' ruck

hey, the chinese are
welcomed into
western civil-i-beast
ATTEN 'Hut!

And this metaphor was a wild cry
from the captive
tit-bird's throat!
Christmas beer christmas queer
that the wild-man
hunched & bound 'n
chains
brought the quiet
man down
with a whim 'n a wish
make my eyes grow fascinated

as I hear wild-man
christmas
song
intoning & praising

the virgin's baby
howling boy!

III
Wild-Man Eats Christmas Cake

Righteousness
these are good! Birds & Fish
Other beings (prana)
i p u t t h e j
back (prajna)

Wild-man had Cristmas dinner today
Wild-man leaves
the h out
Yes!

Wild-man gains enlight

EnMENT!
he sees the top
of China

spies a Christmas tree
studded with demonic ornaments
bear's green guts & eyes of Bengali

snake-children. Illusion
knows Me. O Joy. Christmas cake & I'm
intent on salvation

Weapons do not break him/ H E R O heaven?
Christmas cake.
the single moment
of passion
is superior to dead 'time'

Wild-man eats Christmas cake & thrusts
a lit candle
at the sky.
He screams: "He is alive!"

A quiet breath, Compassion/
Wild-man finishes up the crumbs
of Christmas cake.

Quiet bliss. Obedience.
I cannot tell thy
Praise!

IV
Wild-Man and the Woman of the Stony Cave

When we come
say the old women   we come as ugly
as possible.
not to give the men illusions
of perfection   lest they stuff feathers
in their gullets

& rage against the fate
that sent them a wild-woman
wearing a wooden leg.

O wild-man
smash his eye-lids

against the picture
of the woman with a
mask & a wooden leg.
a black-eyed
st. Barbara
vomiting up incense
& bread
her anger causes
the fatal
death of farm animals/

wild-man
swore
at HaLlelulYahs &
praises to jesus
he thought of
torturing the
DIVINE MIND
O choke on feathers!
O choke on satan's glass eye!
O let the hairy raging
woman curse
the stony caves & bang her crazy leg
of wood
in a wedding dance!

V
Wild-Man on a Monday Nite

look Up
build an altar be sleepless
/O Lord. Hide me near a well/ I whack
at the mystery

wild-man   served   God

He ware a Holy Doktor

he grew near the
sea.   Beloved   or filthy dog
he said.

what am I/
I Am That I Am/
wild-man taught wisdom & shared his bed
with All.
His fiery body
belched golden grace/
diamonds
stuck on
his/
tongue.
He hewed down a cross
in his head.
For we are to urges
as Satanic
lips/
caress
baldy angels.
I Am The Lord, I Change Not.

Where my head points   I smear
all the doorknobs with blood/
grape Juice
is so acid
it stings
my lips
wild-man smiled on Monday
nite.
He hath smeared all the doorknobs with blood.

VI
Wild-Man Sees the Vinegar Rainbow

vinEgar
burns a forehead
what's the serious
CAUSE
did a magician do it?
tho/ught wild-man.
heaven attracts
the ordered destiny
now separate now come

toGETHER
WILD
watermelons
spew
ferocious blood.
I am altogether yours—
sings wild-man
let me eye you he begs

he's like a crazy slave
.he falls on
his knees/
too hard

much much predictable pain
blood-sticky rain making things grow
smoothest garlic
bulbs of the
world.
O Animal EYE
does wild-man belong both to

god &
the evil hour?
which themes speak clearest meaning?

wild-man says:
do you talk too much?
He sees the angel Gabriel squeeze

—a horse head.

VII
Wild-Man Counts His Perfections

Here he comes
Wiping Out Evil
he EScapes
to our houses
/exHAUSted
he brings forth children
little climbing insane dwarfs
with cold lips/
wild-man
says "I want
a virgin"
to spin in a dance
her navel like a winking eye

I suck it & move about
her beautiful & noble fleisch!
Wild-man pays pennies for ritual
& poetry
a bed on the black earth/
he rests & eats cherries
/swearing against dwarfs, dogs, U.S.
presidents, gestures of terror, sex acts
of a SECRET SOCIETY
the imprint of his cock
forced into black tar

whatever color he loves   he eats/
purples & fuscia   green & violet
giggling yellows   he madly
loves/
he calls them stars!

what perfection is the bone
in my foot   what a beautiful
day
/what is the master's name?
I abhor the
strength   for killing   but I Am
a wild-man!

VIII
Wild-Man's Day B'fore New Year's Eve

wild-man made
Catherine die
she defiled
him/
he remembered the
reddish haze around her head.
Christ caught between the laundry room &
the incinerator
/he was doing
earthly chores/ nor does wild-man
remember
the tangerine they shared each
with t'other

the two naked bodies
eternalized by the sacred
polaroid.

he had taken pictures of her
bent over a bundle of clean bed sheets
/smelled as pure as two bathed shepherds/
ass glowing near
violet burning candles
.smells
of warm grape clusters/
wild-man wearing a
helmet & carrying the cross,
facing the large window
lips smiling &
honey-gleaming
tongue spurting
miraculous prayer

/ his hands hold a book
of blessings & images of golden balls
/Christmas.
3
temple
prostitutes
sing
praises &
AILeLuHiA!

IX
Wild-Man's Busted Beer Bottle

wild-man says he hears
the sky freeze
he feels like a
KING
/it's new year's eve
& he knows

that he
ALONE
has
revealed
the peacefulness of
the constellations

a roach body bleeds under the
heel of his foot/
"once upon a time 'twas a drop
of lust" sings wild-man
& Now it dead & gone.
i look away & feed
my eye THE MOON
/ passion PoEtRy

.standing quiet the devil opens a hole
i look into it/
a filthy cuckoo book
O wild-man cries FEAR NOT & GIRD THY
LOINS!
he walks away. clasps a finger
to a finger tells his neighbors
that he has tweaked the tits
of movie stars UNDERSTOOD THE SYSTEM

of the Universe/
stood fascinated smelling
the rhubarb
nr the sea/
never thinking of WAR &
floods.

X
Wild-Man's Common Truth on New Year's

it's significant
that I lay open bear's head. nor do you
protest! I do MY will.
Am I Not Wild-man?

every Hand shakes against me
because of MY
TRUTH/
I speak!
You can trace it to Tibet.

once I overcame dogs racing in the woods.
SWine taught me the Art of War / no one knows
my writings/
Did The Master have
ten ears?

I Hate poverty. Gold & jade you can
choke on / Amber will give you a clear voice
You CAN SCREAM:
I HAVE A CLEAR VOICE!
You can say hairy, white, liver
BLACK
bride with a
rash.
Still the World is not yet
at peace.
the man walks in tar
with his brother Music is the
Light going out
the freeing
of the loved one.
the Corpse has the
sharp/Est ears.

I
See
a Myriad
of Evil
WOrlds!
—sang wild-man.

XI
Wild-Man's View-Eye of the Blessed

in its downward
(heaven)
course
/yet left apart from the
LAST COLD
the key to the Universe
stood upright in THE blood

Water & fur
he needed
for his whole meanings
Divine Reason
was the Good growth of Holy
Plant
completely pure
O Creator!
sang Wild-man/
I shall fulfill
& press my hands against
burning center.
Death contradicts
earth/heat/Sun
viscous damp leaf
borning itself.

The name rules air & fire/
the seeking
half monkey face/
separating
dry violent/
Wounds
the desert
the lifted
ancient
Soul
of
/morning.
O evil is fresh &
without Me —sang
wild-man.

XII
The Birth of Wild-Woman and/or the Change

Pressed the foot
on the sand
& He/ Became
Mother
Grey Water were her
eyes
Thumbs pressed in to
INNER BODY
/She screamed
I am soft body
My eyes are green My Hair is white

what is MY Name?
I Play
I Am a Great Thing I exist
woman

woman woman woman pour milk for Isis
Angela
Myrna
wild-woman
Her secret
bells
flamingo singing
lion howling
Surely tomorrow
She will speak
& break twigs/
cherries & apples fall
to
their
death. wild-woman
smokes
His
last cigar
& laughs
in the
sweet morning.
her first day
alive.

XIII
Wild-Woman Sharply & Triumphantly Watches

woman is a Wild
scientist O Lord! Questioning
& going forward like a raving nightingale
/beneath the big-bellied sun
she forces down the
rain.
wild-woman after her own
swirling creation remembered the

miracle
of the Nile running indeede
the river was faythful.
Full of fruit.
she was so rational on Sunday
sitting/
feeling her senses & passion
Over all
the World
Herself Now One
. Unpitied.

to be Part of Tragedy & laugh. Watch
elephant copulate inspiring holy love
keeping the public
/ at peace.
O Woman Innovator! O Self! O languid Messiah!

She plucks out the weeds With
a little finger/
Proud of her
gleaming Mind on the angel's head. Her
dominion/
& She erect
With a loud Voice
Sings Al l
L eLuHIA!
What Virtu is her permanence
her Truth
breathing out
the sacred
minutes/
She grasps a voluptuous
thighed
Stripling

O an angel!
O an angel! & walks with him to
the river.

XIV
Wild-Woman & the Vegetation

air-Boy she called him.
He spit at her missing the frog. Paradise
is this green front part of my Eye/ She thought he
whispered
I rub against the slab/
of forest Wood
I will write my name on the parchment
I will call myself Woman-Abraham
my mouth uncovers
Prayer/ Her wounds spurt milk
Her angel
balances
himself with
a Cross
shaped in
Water. Greed Greed Greed/
She watched herself in the
water

chicken necks & backs
glistening & turning into garlands of
jewels from
Babylon
O she would flow down
the edge of
the River
Death grotesque & cunning
would
offer her money & she
would disturb the
water
& shatter
it into Flames/
Where is the vege

tation I want to
smell & touch
small flowers
. pulled wide. laughing
Vulva.
I am your solace!
Sing me to my sacred grimace!

XV
Wild-Woman & the Daemon in the Water

3 passions gave her help/
The arrows tempted
the fish – – – Her
flesh risen Over
her sacred feet
delightful sing Oing.

.Water defines
beginning middle & E N D

her EYES would begin
The pilgrimage to the C E N T E R

of first human
touching fish/ a crown
a crown a crown & another woman
in the storm
/O false drooling
golden-eye Demon
afternoon fiend
sharing a pork sandwich

may you drown in water.
thru love & grace may water run in your stomach sac
pushing forth pride/
fur coat mania
& lechery!
Wild-woman saw herself as Grey-beard
for one minute carrying a pack of gold
& blasting a horn/
the angels running like foxes kissing each other
tasting the gritty chins
meek & slipping
in new animal shit/
laughing & laughing * O gleaming
brain of woman-Abraham
She has Made the
devil Chop Off/ himself
& drink a
cool glass of water

. suck a little soap

XVI
Wild-Woman Sitting in the Center of Water

in honour of her/ the wild-woman
Esther of woman!
O wild star with an iron ring eating water O she
the graceful wizard
/& she floats with
Animals
in water. She digs
her curious
fingers into clay. Clay cries

thou Art the criminal!   See what
light splits beneath shadow.

Big Shit Fish Gives no warning—
when it turns around your snatching hands!
O cry fish   stop!   smile your eyes
10,000 times so that the fish
lick her face   /sweet.
wild-woman
Saw the Profound Cave
it has no beginning to the beginning
it has glory in its thirsty opening/ no greater
laughter
than the cracking shoot of light/
O nature of light!

There she found no retribution   No burning of green
plant & fish
Sound handed
& walking to her   everything
feeling like the yolk of an egg.
what is
religion?   fishes shaking
in her blood
/her Mind
linked   To   THE
brittle & ancient
fish-trap   foul
reeking leather.
Her lawful Spirit.
Her on the edge
of earth.
O Wild-woman sitting in the Center!

from

Shemuel

(1979)

Baroque Blister Song

let me eye You
whistling during an evil hour
the dying fish
is the clearest Meaning

the Black
Savage Burning moving 1
Square

suffocation

on

the worlde's Surface

the Mind
of the blood.

Eliot's Blister Song

old brain
Selah the levels
of The Enfolding
& then what
cuts back?
what does it mean
this technological
blood-sticky rain

I See the Angel Gabriel
give
solace

the Meaning cleanses
the violence
to
birds

Milton's Blister Song

What is the color of
the flowing Worlde

death-dove

a forest of Ripening
death

apples
breast-rib

earth unites water

the Bangkok cats piss

all grass is the same the
jackals blacker than
a gasp

tiny oranges cells bright split
like chalk the legs of workers
horse-fly the memorable vulgar
sunset now we face our acid test
exile

point out that 220 million see
visions 10 million see drought
this country huddles beneath
banana trees kerosene and cement
                                        bleakest
nepotism colossal 13 million
sharp blows then four million
from bangladesh then the war
aging us all alike very vitals
                                        destroyed

                                                            the air force the
left wing
                                    moving the colonels all

crazier than the generals the

truckmen

                                    sucking pipe bombs

Joe's fault
                                    Joe's Fault
                                                                        Joe's pro-
blem he declared his own people

                                    crazier than Congress so

the disturbances we trust fully

before they explode around us we

trust the minister who eats tran

quilizers & zips up his fly with

our family & attorney watching

the Act

mr sincerity loves country music
that i didn't dream about in
the sunshade faces woken up
damn fid dler watch out brother
50 years ago a nightrider can
see clearly the childhood of
oppression doub led war song
in repose Uncle Unc le in agony
for catholic men jus t jammed
together anti-semitic q ueen of
sheba finding out she's plain
broke buying used camels &
dried figs flaking off flecks of
salt cod the source of the drago
n of the sinai blue denim large
golden nose-ring our baby from
the land of hittites my former
self itching to get even & then we
t

J. S. Bach's Blisters

blood of the savage

the nose-ring is loved

by the catholics of rome

whistling

& eyeing

the surface of

the negev the jews technological
angel gabriel levels breast-rib
black apple
what is the color

of a gasp

listen to
rollo may
for fear
of cleopa
tra pushi
ng the we
alth of s
udanese
s hits the
farmer kn
ows the p
rice of c
amels & t
ired & an
gry just
picks the
most fant
astic bar
gain & ea
ts his oy
l & olive

why can't i have the shiksa
wailed the queen of sheba why

must it be the descendent of
haile selassie & the original queen

my existence is not forever so
why can't i have the foreign
woman from across the eber why
water unites earth the limit
is boldness so why can't i have

the strange woman thousands &
thousands all grass is the same
jackals let loose their knees
the adventure turns us white
the foreign stranger's breast near

my own the perfection of the
dream receives ripening apples

i deserve even more of a medal
than ezekiel for keeping the f
aith the day of this human rac
e & floor wax
the meaning of ter
rible hiding according to all the
compassion the honor of th
e nations is
skull song cracked
truth the rice flesh is skull
song jeroboam in the land of
egypt & the nest
of spoilers t
he annihilation walking & jud ah
only hallowing & shining t hru
the queen's memory amen d
aughter of his perfection of

dream

it wasn't my fault the drought
it's $40 a year
my rising voice of corruption
i am a moved go
dddddeeesssss i wore wool pais
ley saris with
a vest of idealism my brother
is an autoerot-
icist living in france now we
are a nation o
f many famous races everywher
e i would like
a new museum built there is a
drought that i
never would have wanted if i
could have hel
ped it kerosene & cement shor
tages exaspera
te me

my fallen shrine is
woolworths they have
retired it's presiden
t

what now in multi-to
ne do you expect to g
ather anywhere the num
b
er of deaths is bent
on hell without succe
ss last week only hour
s
to go the ju ry inter
viewed the task force
because of tape worms t
h

e men were not relieve
ed

the politicians like good
wardrobes a goldfish with
fire in his eye one of the
nice things is the boast
of a leader he says i am
38 years old & i know what
pakistan feels like i could
touch the genitals of the
new baby country forever
what do you want from me
mother teresa of albania
she's well-publicized like
tom flanagan from the uni
versity of california who
reflects the silver minnow
in his naked rib-cage

night work that night there
were several strikes 13 dollars
the pregnant woman of ireland

stole who was a cleaning woman
mother of four children the
numbing one was in the jail-

house & resented the health
& bad history in the working-
class district on end for years

many outside the buildings cried
for the sickness in the government
building i found two children

huddling together in the cold
night her own child has no family
her toes are gnarled vaguely she talks

outside
many
who were stolen

of 13 dollars

outside the bad history

of sickness the night work

& the gnarled

toes dig

into the eyes

of irish jack the prize

fighter of finally no reasons

very blue eyes

she scrubs toilets
her anxiety ringing

she's trying to
get more drinks down her

cleaners union
he hit her in
the churning
body the room
smells of americans
they verily say

in cooperation
with the cooperation
of the union of
civic automobiles
we wish to stunt
the growth of

your gentle unborn
children so that
the government of
cyprus will know
a pub from a hole
in the ground.

The Dance of the Bracelets

queen shemuel
investigated the prophets
she pulled punches with prophets
bored into the horny side of prophets

queen shemuel
played ball with the prophets studied
the phenomena of propane gas
a world of illusions
the dizzy prophets the Voice

of something
queen shemuel uttered words of praise

for the prophets
who dazed the whole of america
who sucked the eyes
out of the sockets

the sweeper is poor payed
the corruption is making a
speech
the scandler is payed
poor
the diaspora man named
eleazor katz is poor payed
he kept his coat on
when he prayed
the plan is
to slow down
the poor payed ones

to work like the chinese
across the river eber
henry garcia established
blood mixing with the children of ur

lower lips scandaling
the judges of the community like pigs
with jewels in their snouts
the sophisticated leaders
fewer than 10,000 assessed by municipal

officials during the terrible
wave of heat from across the
river declared a class of
negroes any negro sitting there
a king

i would like a sports car
to nestle in said queen
s hemuel the pipik of a
man from gaza to sport
fish w ith dogs cats a cat
named mehmedbasich
giving relie f's blessing
enough to su pport a
life-time i insis t that
trucks contain 20 tons
of prepared beef from
the land of the medes & s
lippers of a sturdy mater
ial that will not rot in the
desert something that
really works for a change

yes the uproar in memphis
was a limitation stemming from
monday night yes & yes
when mr. kim renewed his
quantitative improvements & sprinkled
travelers with 100 year dragon's balls
yes when mr. chin in chengtu
laughed & with an astro chart strongly
recommended & surprisingly shifted the
embrace of his new perspective
yes & yes
& he found that the unruly youth
dedicated himself to frequent thievery
yes & yes in szechwan

there is no right control
there is only duke elling
ton & his orchestra there
is no leftist cultural re
volution there are only s
ocial leaders & the selec
tion of rooms & the hong
kong credentials of the n
o. 1 man particularly the
commissar in szechwan
& i n chengtu & in
memphis & in belfast
& in the land of haman
the evil for 10 dollars a
night you can s ee them
all in a comforta ble
bathroom with a telep
hone & electric fan

who can know what
they do in gaza or
edom
  in a minute
one can know
    one can know
in a minute if a
woman is fallen
  one can know
in a minute if
a man betrays his
brother
  one can know
in a minute if the
people love the lord

became
known
absolving
she hit him
in the corrupt body
became known
fully cursing
he hit her in the
scary eye
absolving
faster than a
whoring son of mr. yin
faster than a
fly eats honey
absolving
within the letter
the spirit of the
law

i put my other report
in the treasure hour
of the lord i witnessed
the nuptials of a
daughter of mr. yin
i watched the bizarre
bathing of her shaded
areas by concubines
i violated the pits
of her toes with my
sheeps tongue
the angel of death
scorned me among
the sons of men
i became campaign
treasurer in gad
the sons of ishmael
tickled my fancy

The Smell of Apples

by the negev
what is the color of a
gasp   what is the color of
apple   breastrib
black apples or
the nose-rings loved
by the python-lipped sons of
ishmael
sarah's eye
levels
earth has grass & bangkok cats
snake has heat
behind the rusted
jaws
snake sez   whyfore ye die for
judea t'aint all grass the same
besides make yer covenant with me
takes just seconds

the smell of apples
by the negev
the color of a gasp
is the color of apple
the rusted nail
behind black apples
breast-rib &
nose-rings
drool of samael
evil archangel
crippler dabbler in
tin nipples & python
lips of onan &
hysteria of sons
of ishmael

what could be
worse the
snake of course

        yezer is nothing
        the strange god
        between one part
of the eating heart
        the eating heart parts
        apple-soul
        tooth/technique
        yezer is ridicule
        of the sage
        the bowels of nothing
        yezer is nothing
        produced
        the gas of the
        compulsive one
strange god is evil yezer
        nothing is yezer
        but yezer

            possible the guerrillas
            possible the jurists
            possible the gnats
            possible the camels
            possible the millions of
tons of bombs
            possible the front pages
            possible the social revolutions
            possible the american policies
            possible the country's actions
            possible the light dawns

on governments
                possible the mental testing
                possible the facts are unknown
                possible the shoddy thinking
                possible the little or nothing
                possible the taxpayer a scapegoat
& a sheep's ass

moloch
god twist & slant
redemption & let them
steal out of door-locks
joe's city is new york
let pale hand of
infamous canaanite
Lo eighty hands steal
your door-locks
a bony thumb twist
your tits
so that you bend your knee
to me & seek me to
whisper a consolation
to thee
but i scorn thee
thou hast made a pact
with a golden goat
& there can be no peace
between us

again i say let
a piss-hued hand of a
hot greedy canaanite
to eighty stinky hands

steal
with a bony thumb hooking
like a harlot's eye
into your door-lock
& may your enemies
dance a circle dance
& serve milk to the
thieves that slay
your heart
because you listened not
to my voice
may you bend your knee
to a dumb goat
& scream in a jackal's
song
i am saved i am saved

let pale hand of
infamous canaanite
Lo eighty hands steal
a bony thumb out of
new york door-locks &
let the eighty hands
of canaanites seek a
redemption & let them
kill the evil yezer
that modifys my words
so that the words let
no gods before me be
worshipped
shift & twist & slant &
alter to
worship a hundred gods
before me & tho
you bend your knee to
moloch thou art righteous
& saved

so yesterday
they yelled
traiganlo para fuera!
so we can hang
him from the pipes

we identify him as the
treacherous one
he never fully
explained how
he came to be

one of us/
today in the press
they said i was
against myself
how crazy

the one i'm against
is you & so
i cast my fate
with
myself

queen shemuel said
it comes from the law
it comes from the law
it comes from the law
it comes from the law
it comes from the law

five times

the assumption is enforcement
the assumption is enforcement
the assumption is enforcement

the assumption is enforcement
the assumption is enforcement
seven times

the assumption is enforcement
the assumption is enforcement

now everything's accurate

and be fined
mr. yin said
in mexico city
you were the key
dealer in opium
you killed in
olden china
& now you are
the third alleged
fiend driving
in an automobile
containing in the
trunk 264 pounds
of the effecting
drug/ next you
will want a private
plane to fly you
to the nether world
so you can curb
the flow of the
craving demons of
samael

my vulva is nicer
said miriam
my vulva is nicer
said sheba
my vulva is nicer
said cleopatra
my vulva is nicer
said deborah
my vulva is nicer
said dinah
my vulva is nicer
said jemimah
my vulva is nicer
said leah
my vulva is nicer
said the shulamite
my vulva is fatal
said rachel

my vulva is nicer
said sheba
my vulva is nicer
said leah
my vulva is nicer
said dora
my vulva is victorious
said doloris
my vulva is nicer
said cleopatra
my vulva is nicer
said jemimah
my vulva is sweeter
said rita
my vulva is great
said fate
my vulva is fatal
said rachel

i will go in unto her
i will go in unto her
i will go in unto her
i will go in unto her
i will go in unto her
i will go in unto her
i will go in unto her
i will go in unto her
i will go in unto her
i will go in unto her
i will go in unto her
i will go in unto her
i will go in unto her
i will go in unto her
i will go in unto her
i will go in unto her
i will go in unto her

            shemuel the queen
      said—go ask
someone else
                  to fast with you
                  rest your head
                  on a great stone/
                  stone your head
                  on a great stone/
                  you did not fast
                  so stone your head
                  go to a great stone
                  rest your head
                  they will stone you
                  they will want to/
                  ask anyone
                  they will want to
                  sacrifice you for the sake
                  of heav'n

& the city joe woe joe's
city

this is joe's city
wretched city cast
your hooked eye
the slanting nose of a
harlot
left none without
a fuck
them on the edge of a
nipple
the edge of a sword
in the land
of mizpah
on the border of
og mr. yin
on the edge of a
nipple
there is rest from
war

shemuel the queen
said—go ask
someone else
to fast with you
rest your head
on the great stone
stone your head
you did not fast
they will stone you
ask anyone
they will want to

sacrifice you
for the sake of
heav'n
& the city
joe
woe joe's
city

from

Constructs

(1985)

The Surrounding Black-edge

Joe's book of constructs the fortified
core   tanks full of fish   spineless   a
sleeping grub   as usual you stain the wood
three times   and ten days ago fusion begins
the light small on a fishing village   and
Joe said to   the house looking spineless
into the direction of the sun   the water
a luminous road jesus named   the fishing
village   Enfeh   the village is named for
small hair found on the spiny fish famous
for good eating Enfeh dogs skip along the
bay   the surrounding area alarming the
world with   women in white sheets is the
fact bare dogs and horses thirst on the sand

Plaster Angle

Plaster angle   so when you use the machine
follow Joe's line she passed the boundary
it is movable you know   from knives by a
bird's eye to the project wherever it's
located   grinder spray-equipment   your best
buy   many times over Joe became Rose   the
constructs offsetting the limitations now
stepping along glacial time like a   paintbrush
a book of ideas for wiping stain on bare wood
to smooth off wire edges   thought chore   sill
door   into open grain mind   hollow wall use
on the cloudiest day limitless   to darken
out of the way rims speed the destiny of suns
with a level   jewels   save yourself   the edge

Become Limulus

control soil 900 degrees martian soil light
red biological sampling and the sky bluer
the outpost black and white why there is no
tuesday expected as much atmosphere become
limulus like what used to be called science
fiction the life experiments not decisive
imaginings planetary blueprints the birds
manmade womansimilar present to the clear
swirl data gained tuesday night this chilling
outsight of decoys for duplicating the blind
newborns so they can digest the nutrients be
reddish that oxygen prevent the black grackles
the first evidence of killer birds today sees
the heat and high pressure and the malfunction

On Center of a Blue-white Sea

close range in migration and winter   this
bird guide to the house the favored spot
round the base   the construction of Joe's
efforts   striped bird on grey-flesh legs
tell the splitting wood of 100 years hence
that the poet Joe was here   to sell you a
bill of goods   sound one side to the other
hill-side   around the ring-bill of the dove
is the real-estate owner's fork aready to
hitch his good luck to a star-crossed bird
on center of a blue-white plate two birds
to a dinner woe to the woman who does the
dirty work of pinching a mourning dove's
graceful sliding neck   slow dirty work today

In Dead Corners

skin off the insulation   detail   save
time   keep some rivets loose in your
hands   ready to screw   wise plywood
chisel socket exterior repairs fuse and
change the spelling sprayer next day fog
spray your hair sailing light buttery
green lead along the way the road to the
woman   experiments on grain   at bottom
of skilled work excavation building joint
bled circuits include wind rain iron
water   tight cement excess place the
existing mortar

The Wasps in the Door-jamb

here absolute of a turned tall grass
the scratching in the passive wood flung
under the pines   the tall grass hides
and think of the wasps living while you
keep house and past the precision edge
the iodine cleanses the chance of recovering
as poetry sire desire we discover beyond
the dialog the rage the sobbing but what's
cheap wood at the bottom of the door and
the surface sees like a white body a song
languid mercury destroys itself as if you
didn't know

A Doorway or a Breastbone

panels are nailed interior posed if
the house suggests rust at an angle
but to your temper like Joe's so quick
to anger opening up a doorway or a
breastbone the bird spineless never
a gull the fury of Paul edging over
his dying reaching the edge the method
of his poems the metallic green springs
feeling spinning the remote resemblance
to the sea-gulls jack-the-ripper of
birds plotting the robbing of nests
the white of the eye of elohim who sees
all acts the dark patterns constant across
with a high curved ridge the screams

The Edge on the Scarecrow

z minus the straight-edge level diagonal
curve cutting fill all nail holes the
material is needed for life concentrated
light light concentrated for two wooden
housed housed to the base of spine spineless
the walls of the house sing yet it retains
silence thinned to the foundations can
be driven to the depth these slightly thick
fears have plenty excess as usual you
stain the edges with whiteness it's best
to tap the trees on warm days so continue
to tap the trees with a leg over a sleeping
grub narrowing cracks shaped overalls a
scarecrow dipping and slamming against the
wind

Joe's Former Visions

blend out   white enamel the birds steal
the birdlings screams white enamel blend
out the anguish the underside   of riding
praying mantis other small creatures of
Joe's former visions   basement walls of
cups paste and glue never let a   simple
formula rule ya if ya can help it Joe's
advice to windows and doors of summer vinyl
drives suggest you never hang the overalls
directly in the sun   burn them in the
furnace see if Joe cares   dusty slow pain-
staking work is all that has been changed
spineless I count on the calls of screaming
parent birds   same way the old one did

Migrates through East

pink mauve   folds concentrates bone
edge considering sailing the third winter
before the icefloes   roses for   the black-
iris eyed important food gatherer depth int-
erruptions   a wave of the hand   and the
other hand cups   seeds that the birds use
the upturned chin of the cat   seen by
the audiovisual concentrated group   or
farther west   summer   herring   white ibis
migrates through east   the elegant bowl
of the glass   and knuckles against harsh
white cotton pants   lying in dried grass

Herring

iceland   white indian harsh cotton pants
much wind it will pull   the first winter
from below show that your laughter throughout
lasts thru the second winter   a stone or pumice
breaking   without rocking   the space saw
cuts the surface of concrete forms brick
stone   the herring is black line on white
current blending carefully with the hardened
glue sheet to tube joints keen in light passes
through the house 100 years future will the
peeled orange white fibers fixated on the
corneas memory   the cotton pants in the sun

Two Deer

white indian harsh   the two deer panting
much wind will pull   down thy hates   cotton
tail rabbits saw the forms   first   that
100 years fixated on the corneas   memory
not relative   a stone or broken pumice
grained into the sand   the space cuts the
line of the movements of the two deer
running   the peeled white orange   resting
in the delighted hand of a girl   who watches
cotton just washed pants in the sun   the
dried glue to tube joints in the light
music of jazz and bob-o-link   visual

Kiss from the Fuel Cylinder

the units end   tools
wiring stripping   two metal
cylinders about right now surface
source san francisco   pantomime
scrap stock determine 45 degrees inward
nails will chip knives work won't touch
edge bottom edge bottom edge bottom
work of cut of each time   tools
three metal no surface   well enough
for the deer in the other poems to
gambol leaping about in dynamical frolic
use a medium speed hal   ting look with tears

Latex Examined

this is just a rag tightness spin
progressively as the terminal   home
mechanic is working on it if she needs
the sun o k the starting problem is
fixed by fresh oil the dust because on
the restored sun etched only a slight
shadow breakdown the graphite sprays
thick and heavy grass cut-down they
should be wood without ox-grease once
a year greasing the mower once a year
applying only a rotary blade encountering
the summer debris thick on the grass

Sandpaper

quite so produce keen edges set sideways
made hard steel like the shroud steals
the final look wears the stone out from
the right of the photograph stone may
jerk work and overheat in a fraction of
time as fire so a powergrinder is a must
even as it slides wood cheaply in that
combination of hand light oily dripping
flat metal you can go on past the precision
or you can go to the middle guard around
the head surface keep tips of fingers to
lessen the chance of scratching

The Winter Saw

to saw wood   to be able to saw wood   signpost
the short dream   in front of the white paper
the consciousness of sawing wood   the activity
of the saw which breaks forth around around
mortifying the ink spot on emily dickinson's
dress the plume in her hat spiked darts an
ornamental array of fox prints on white snow
paws on the brocade divan until the old farm
fence appears again sits up unaware of the
insect changing in the perfect friend's eye-
lid flicker hypnotized by the reflection in
the inkwell silvery grains of salt

Spin Scaffold Lite-blue

do the bird good   ceiling flyward the
extent of the birds span scaffold her
wings in one hand one can paint birds
the way one values birds   wet down next
day fogspray neck spot side stripes spies
the ceiling spineless you do your work
pick up a chunk of pure protein between
eating reflect on where the bald eagle
soars pure soaring imperfect and upside
down as soaring sometimes goes you do
the sharp corner edge of your existence
find the kink or the crook of your life
don't repair it or even re-vision bluish
wings against the contrast of grains

East

long triangle   of the eye   looking at
the base virtually no yellow except what
is rapid living thru the first winter
sun typical phase   like a window trans-
mitting light so bold a pattern   something
like immature moths   do not try to distinguish
the breeding plumage   one motion of eye
window pane planes geometric   upward the
oxygen flows formations swift on the gulf
coast so I do not regard the window coloring
the grey of the rest   the diagram explains
when a stone is tossed into the marsh

Damp Spots on Plaster

power driven brooklyn parkwar between the
boys who grew into   problems they were not
concerned with being the sons of farmers or
at each end of a birthday splitting hedge-
leaves with a finger-nail the girls of weather
cold-sores in the inner nose the membranes wet
and inefficient a foreign insight but vital
as a death-throe of a field mouse or an
infant during damp weather scratching a
finger on a measle leaving a pock on a chin
so that after the last exhalation it will last
a tiny round circle of energy shining shining

from

W.C. Fields in French Light

(1986)

1

A fragment catalog paste-up
of the 20th century
a time lapse
a naive father allegory
She says: The scruples
of myself should be
the scruples of the world
the woman as wrongly treated
as the Nez Percé Indian
Quest of extremes
I'm enamel-eyed
a ritual slaughterer
hypnotized

Alone the lonely poet
lonely as a fish
speaks into the darkness
in the voice of W.C. Fields:
Busy making a device
naturally
this is as the custom determines
But as is the custom
a thing done as that
which was done before
you came along
you rotten kid
The photos of starved African young
hardly stir anyone
The primal Adam says:
My surging, my vitality
my own arms round about me

round about me & a boat
under me, I go roving
with my dark love,
laying up
meat for the holidays

And let your innards
turn to piranha fish
Light of the sunny land
ho ho ho
my own arms holding
the reindeers
voluminous buttocks
I am the St Nicholas
of your nightmares!
This is a law for the west
When looking at photos
of Iwo Jima
I'm reminded that I want
to make you a gift
of my bald head,
my khaki pants
my soldier eye of blue
préférez-vous?
Where would you place
my gentleness?
I'm a rich man, says W.C.
the roads, mountains, skies
& eating rolls on thruways
ain't my cup of tea
Light of the sunny land
ho ho ho
Miles up a solitary gravel
road, miles up a solitary
road, look in my eye
as I whisper
as a lonely poet should
here are some speckled eggs
on neutral gray
And as for French Huguenots
who exactly were they
ho ho ho
but I remember the ladies
graceful arches
indeedy I do
they were gothic-style

The snow is blowing
over Nez Percé despair
a heart of flat space
making a twinge of pain
A tale before doubt
scorpions, the wing-tips
of birds, mutiny,
the last gasp
The tramping American
revolutionary listens
to drenching rain

2

On earth in the territory
of the coliseum
I see you, and you expel from me
my ferocity, my criminal wit
my agility
I spring like a freight-car
made of silk & bullets
I am the male of your dreams
wearing a paste-on-mustache
a halloween child asking you
for candy

An intestine in my body
rises in fear
as the criminal takes my money
Shock suspends the ventricle
the stem chugs up the stomach
the criminal twitches
the exact quantity of energy
for injury & death

I am longing for revolution
iron bar in my hands, my eyes!

Concussion war!
I'm rigid with courage
standing in the place
where the spleen activates
the plot
against my death
I'm speaking into darkness
Take my life, he says,
But give me a kiss

Release my fear when my brain
a big worm stares out
And let me, the American
revolutionary
look at it eye to eye
and not be afraid to die
like Peter Stuyvesant
and George Washington
And remember the Alamo!

Preserve mine integrity
as my life processes
suspend themselves
in the mute choice
of self-preservation
I fall to the sidewalk
I see the luncheonette fluorescent
lights blinking in 3-series
my blood a problem on concrete

The American revolutionary
loves the martyrdom
of St. Sebastian
the erotic saint is
remembered in Brooklyn
The mutilated American
visualizes the internal
organs
quiet as sculpture

Alone, the lonely poet
lonely as a fish
speaks into the darkness
in the voice of W. C. Fields
In the covered wagons of yore
I saw the American revolutionary
gazing blindly & eating
a bowl of pinto beans

All the categories are open
Remember that lest you
dig your teeth in rage
on an old lamb-bone
The permanence of millions
of gallons of earth
The American revolutionary
leaps the abyss

The sacred heart is American revolutionary
razor-voiced, a concrete ikon
biochemical fervor
to make the circle perfect
It's a habit wrought
while I talk

Miles up a solitary gravel road
miles up a solitary road
Snow covers the gasoline pump
The year is dated Earth substance
Outside of this sound
I'm not interested in a totally
professional presentation
I sing with the troubadours
and gasp at the unseen
I smile at the theme
to link American revolutionary
to everything

Next fall I'll fall
for a business opportunity
black oil into the system
the conversion of water
survival technique
kicking my legs out

I am alive whistling a tune
I want to be a living woman
see a tiny caterpillar
waving in the light
As I whisper as a lonely poet
as a lonely poet should
here are some speckled eggs
on neutral gray
Look in my eye
Words & blood animate
Flypaper in summer bungalows
of fifty years ago

The American revolutionary
assaults courtly literature
abstracts it
The assault on courtliness
is as follows:
The American revolutionary
written in the form
of a collective
or a mass-biography
is a study of an individual
in conflict with society
The heroine of the story
emerges first as a bizarre
figure whose goal
is to transform herself
into a poet so that by
asserting her courtliness
she can win a place
in society

by the end of the tale
she stands as a quixotic
individual pathetically
positive to the insistent
mendacity and grossness
of a world which subverts
courtliness

3

The American revolutionary
    is your brother-in-law
wearing better leather clothes
    than you
You appear to others
    bug-eyed in surprise
Whole decades pass
    as bewildered you
deposit messy anxious dreams
    around the house
mortgaged to the hilt
    Ixion New Rubber Hoses
or whatever in soft tones
    and explosives
the birth of envy
    of your brother-in-law
wearing colored incomprehensible
    shrove tuesday italian silk
socks
    God pity you

I am bewildered
around the ascent
of woman
the thinker's wisdom
core of the atom
your own cells
the wind at my forehead

Alone the lonely poet
lonely as a fish
speaks into the darkness
in the voice of W.C. Fields:
Today in the post office
the American revolutionary
received the letter bomb
from Jerusalem.
Who will open letter bombs
today?
Who will stop asking questions
stop the demands of why & who
and open the letter bomb yourself
& who will watch you
from 20 feet away
while your fingertips & nose
fly to the moon
In the 18th century
the bar rooms of the western
pioneer towns stood for
O a different map
of the world unlike anything
you saw
My granddad charting
the connection
to the new world

    You cook on flint today
A line on a chart connects
    like islands point to point
like veins point to old clocks
A guide has been prepared
    the text should prove
itself
    One's own work
Each year on the coarse
    gravel
the revolutionary plants
    her feet

that will be gone
    long after
the fragile bladder
    sinks to humus
and the maidenhair camptosorus
    is at home

The military towns
women of heavy clay
storms riding
the cinnamon ferns irregular
rocks age, woods soak
drawings & plans
poor chipped tooth neanderthal
in palestine stone
between entering heaven
& digging rocks
between dry spells
slow paths
the chips fall

The eyes of the camel-keepers
are the truest
they burn out the sun
The sigh in the desert
is everywhere
the honesty of the breath
of camels
All's well with camels
All's well
There are things
that have
a certain choice
quality
I have six pieces of flint
& a bird

4

The text is behind
the revolution
desperate with imagination
eyelids, the bodily organs,
analytic, figure-making
The solid family-tree
burned out
of mind
cause & effect
these datings
none deserve but the brave

There are two things
that I wish not
to be reminded of
they cause my heels to burn
with shame
& they are more wonderful
& terrible
than an eagle on a rock
or a man with a maid
The day I made a woman weep
at the sight of Albion
& the day
            I promised her
I will wait for you
forever   to step out
of the darkness
quoth the American revolutionary
nevermore

The frog with undivided
single sense
I live it as I have
felt it
Remember little green one
there is no justice

what is killed is left
uneaten
to rot without a psalm
eyes unpenitent
The vivid scream
draws this singer
The virtue is
the beginning of the mystery,
the plagued self with a loud song
Who has made visible bloomed
aquamarine stone?
The visionary
This passionate creation is
the voyage
Slow, a dry land
that I never touch,
to the tune of black tin
whistles,
uneven lash, snowfall
Is love strong without
this old sense?
Stack the phrases
of the ripped palms
of the revolutionary
She will tell the truth
Arrange the twelve poets
'round her

Alone the lonely poet
lonely as a fish
speaks into the darkness
in the voice of W.C. Fields:
Joe thought french
was a fag language
but he knew that
if he didn't have a
resonant twirly voice
he wouldn't sound
like a fag

France needed
a rewriting of
history
The American revolutionary
will change the image
of France in the blinking
of an eye
France needs a new image
the opera and Louis Quinze
and the radical left
are not enough
Joe will cauterize
the effete image
of la belle france
When joe speaks french
you will know he isn't french

5

The courtly lady
of Tang origin says:
My eyebrows kick
little stones
the forms of my heart
are perpetual embarrassment
long before Homer spoke
I could not begin my breath
without shyness
I say 'hi' to everybody
My voice is a prolonged
muscular twitch thick
as an elephant's trunk
When will I develop
into a form?
A circle of whistling
Cassandras-whoosh!

Long before Sappho
kicked grass under a circle
of whistling girls
taken into herself by
folded arms
yellow cats move my eyes
borders of world around
the view beyond
little hills of fertilized
wheat
The elephant's trunk
resounds with the song
of the poet
My voice is one breath
with muscular circles

I can start from the molecule
to the finish of a song,
from a beginning,
in back of a silk purse
sitting in the middle
of ricefields
a whistling girl
with black eyebrows
calling elephants to water

6

It is for me poetry
the essential nucleus
of the sphere of human
existence
Data
that represents primal
things
I shall not do without

precision communication
formalization
I generate example

She gazes at batches
of white roses
white roses
she listens to music
she thinks of white roses
is that not enough?
she thinks of the white paws
of the cat
Sunlight
whirling rose leaves around

A woman in a white shirt
a woman who listens to music
and gazes at batches
of white roses
She is not only of a neat
appearance a woman in
a white shirt but a woman
who listens to music also
and gazes at batches
of white roses Sunlight
whirling rose leaves around
O here comes Balboa
walking the length
of the sea

River bed split
into two singing trees
cross vein
O here comes the rodeo lover
She has a skill blazing
gunplay
O here comes the rodeo lover
fer pete's sake

Look an old sheep
      in new yawk
city what lost its
      teeth
bleeding under the
      fluorescent lights

It's a dwelling place
for her, the cowgirl
she of the dry-storm eyes
thrown from a horse
in a sandstorm
found cradling a dented can
of corned beef hash

      & W.C. said
We will all be sexy zebras
one day, fit
to breed lumberjacks
loyal and sturdy
American revolutionaries

Wagon-trains only are her companions
On the bus she hobbles
in golden stirrups
She's plumb loco
lost in a warehouse hoping
inhaling urgently
the air of laughter
establishing her bravery
in the territory of poets

As George Washington
is a territory of psychological
material
I consider the actor W.C. Fields
my gangplank
to walk from one world
to another

Cowboy working in a gas-
station, stubbly chin,
smashed in cafeteria,
old-freezed apple pie
I consider W.C Fields
actor prayer-book talking
cement bronc-buster
In the bridal chamber
work is progressing
by big boss American revolutionary
W. C Fields eating
fort knox g-string

Short-trigger gunman
in rodeo, W.C's the best
as I am best in drama
and as guest of honor
moseying in the smoky
medieval halls of Chaucer
W.C. and me in the movies
talking loudly
sticking our stiff shovels
into the reactionary hopes
of Americans,
loading up in the rough
country
our own power

I am not oblivious
to free words, blizzard-choked
I wander
bound by the rules of poets
washing gold down my throat,
then twenty-one phone calls
to Fields,
writing my name on the stirrups
of his riding self
Now there's a scene change
I am a fat show-business producer

with cigar
And W.C.'s an out-a-work actor
His lips are playing tricks
with the tip of my corona
Now he's very glib
and begging me for work
                for words, a fight,
                    a gun, a chance
                to be my irish father
                    He's earned
                pocket-digging
                    vug rust-eater
                sluicer, irish orphan
                    twist oliver
                he's paid his dues
                    Poignant he claims
                he's earned his bit o'pain
                    So lemme alone
                W.C. sez
                    He asks why
                I write poems about him
                    I ask 'why not?'
                You're a myth
                    & I intend
                to utilize you

A horse-dealer in America
A collector of shoe-boxes of poems
by the American revolutionary
Myself, a loquacious woman
rises above the mountains

I tell W.C. to cut off
the edge of his heel
for love of me
I say, 'you are my glory hole,
my mine, my gold field
& the poems I make
will cause crumbling & erosion
of the world'

7

1776 the living 200th year
out of the ark the dove flies
The American revolutionary
Barbara Fritchie says:
Like a child dangling a lizard
from her hand
Here is a cruel sociological
fact, you are the first
perfection, the only right
child
Hear my poignant
claim
Guard it

Drink to savages of increase:
These bones sing move along
without a theory
Simple with creation
the art of longings

Thus spake the child
I know where the garden is
the stock exchange zoo
the cemetery
But what is this building
for but to lean against
near a bus-stop
What is that rope for
but to hang from
The entrance, the way out?

And Barbara Fritchie says
It is right
that the revolutionary
perseveres
Then the meaning is fluid
to a close

We're still here in America
Where is the meeting place
for strangers
of bright kimonoed poets?

Alone, the lonely poet
lonely as a fish
speaks into the darkness
in the voice of W.C. Fields
I lay bricks & make
plastic belts also
jazz tapes,
I name the dozens of countries
that I want to visit,
wearing a mask
that seals the sight
on the final afternoon
We're finished
riding on the gray horses
to cold regions

8

Bulletin.
Yesterday the Algerians
scheduled a demonstration
at Sacré Coeur
Who lived in hope
Abraham an Algerian
with an extraordinary
ability for jumping ship
The hard part is
catching up with 'em
Riding on a peugeot
bicycle is food
for thought

In Paris his memory
of Algiers
as religious as
Sacré Coeur

Decapitated chickens
are found on rue du Bac
Slaughterers
on rue du Bac
What a wonder on
rue du Bac
                Patterns.
The environment transferring
elements,
rough male mythology
four hours a week two
hours a day the henna-haired
women of Algerian origin
sliding on the surface
waters of european
socialism

9

She fell back
the warped one
He drew circles
She died at the hands
of fifty warriors
The army saw them
at Sacré Coeur
They joined her
up at the hill
like a flock o' birds
over Sacré Coeur

Two calluses a day
on my one foot,
a coral reef hard
as food production
in undeveloped nations,
a potential source
of tiny sea animals
plankton

I'll learn how
to say Sacré Coeur
perfectly like beans
cooking in a pot
of black iron
My voice will be
wonderful
I'll develop patterns,
flux & structures
It will be marvelous
photo-regulation,
a respiratory metabolism
that is the rosy
perfection of two hours
of my life every week
learning french
entertaining myself
at a meeting of
acid-rain analysers
& sliding on the floors
in the perfumed casbah
of Sacré Coeur O
Sacré Coeur O
Coeur O Sacré

Yearning
for good rabbit meat
the elite Egyptian
in low tones
explains the conversations

of Algerians
who rue the day
they left that inhibited
dusty town outside of
Algiers

Who rues the day
they left their
inhibited dusty town
to strike out!
O hometowns of no
rabbit stew
and the wrath of oil-kingdoms
triple-edged electric signs

And W.C. said:
Listen to my jargon
I like to look at you
The lure of your
arched nostrils
capture me
When you are in
the process of purifying
yourself
with blue bathoil
the logic of the world
is in the color
of the rhythm
of your hands

When you thieve
my money-belt
I absorb the electricity
of the movements,
your stereo-sinews
don't let me down

As for poetry
I greatly admire

W.C. Williams
and his two flossies
for the price of one
Two flossies for the price
of a good doctor poet
a good doctor of boyish
charm is worth a festival
of flossies
A gaggle of girls
in a state of ecstasy
female dementia
described by compassionate
doctor
What has the name
of a dog
Whistles asthmatically
and does capers?
And makes the best
cabbage salad in town
And makes the best
cabbage salad in town
Patterns.
Of patronized women

The dramatic blood
combining the letters
moving forward
the penetrated cells
the bony lower jaw
in pure line split
like a wax crayon
In the absence
of searching
I could've danced
all night
Dancing the way I think
Bursts forces coincidence
My voice does not exist
outside of amazement!

10

Who is lounging
on rue du Bac
in the morning after
strange disillusionment?
Head bulging like a wine bottle
in a sailor's hand
Crisis, danger, chronic sickness
the future?

I am standing
looking into the sun
on rue du Bac
My white mane flying
I'm the river ghost
of a mystical landscape
I wither, vulnerable,
a sad catholic in madrid
A supreme obstruction—
the last part disliked
by myself
All beautiful white electricity
to run down myself

I speak french
to the surface temperature
My eye is a rock
The second year will see me
dynamic as the blue ridge
mountains of virginia
My gift will be
an intensive course
in the Fine Art of the evening
and social revolution
Cognitive thinking is thinking
to a spider & Everything Else
What a triumph at Sacré Coeur!

A sword of my word
shapes Sacré Coeur
bends the sentence
into rock
I look out of
the arabian desert, listening
I create the scroll, the mirror
of the normal
I see the body
My attention is mystery
& claim
While waking & lying down
& walking to & fro

Brooklyn Turf Odessa

Grandmother.   I've
made the curry for
9 mouths I would suggest
a coffee break
Deliver unto me O Lord
prime father o'er
the suez canal,
an overtime job—
to do nothing all day
but evict rich landlords
There was an old woman
who lived in a shoe
poor as a catholic
poor as a jew
there was an old woman
who lived in a shoe
with mangled womb
& an eye of blue

For me.   You color
the world for me
I am tenacious
in my awe
of how
you color the world
for me
There was an old woman
who lived in a young woman
who lived in an old woman
For me
you color the world
for me

I am tenacious
in my awe
of how
you color the world
for me
who lived in a shoe
poor as a catholic
poor as a jew

Itzhak
Isaac
laughter
sob

Itzhak
Isaac
laughter
no job

Itzhak
Isaac
whiskey
sob

Itzhak
Isaac
laughter
no job

Itzhak
Isaac
baby son
Itzhak

Isaac
sugar bun
Itzhak
laughter

Isaac
whiskey
laughter
whiskey

Grandfather.   He was
curious about social justice
& not just whiskey
& he had premonitions
about destructive
leadership
He dreamed of a
long postponed trip
to Paris
Sliding on the floors
of Sacré Coeur
C'est bon
C'est bon
C'est bon

Once grandfather
in dark robes

in a motel in Danzig
lay with Johanna Iscobwitz
cheese-cheeked & pumpkin-
headed on a beach in Capri
winking & connecting with
lady pudenda
Grandmother Etta guaranteed
that he was a rattlesnake
In Czechoslovakia
they called grandpop's deeds
"bold opportunism"
I myself clash
with that image—
the pressure of grandpop's
horny legs in the early
afternoon
Johanna Iscobwitz
wondering whether
he would really
join the forces
of social change
She sought to aid
his demand of nine
bottles of whiskey
& they occupied
the silky vestibule
of Sacré Coeur, Coeur O' Sacré
Sacré Coeur in the sleepy
afternoon O Sacré Coeur
Coeur of Sacré
I'm the one
who bought the dinner
committed voyeurism
with Johanna Iscobwitz
Dropped to my knees
in a flowered-wallpapered
motel & searched for flies
on the toes of Johanna

I let my children cry
uncaged like canaries
nagging around
the lower part of Brooklyn
O bring your hunger
to nowhere,
my children
my super energy-depleters
You drive me insane
when you grab my whiskey
Call me grandpop
Let us create
a viable relationship
What will you think of next
if you wish me dead
I am the oldest son
drifting nowhere
Someday you & I
will take a trip
to Tangier

Be careful
Calculate
O when I was born
on tuesday
found out it was a
thursday
Memory of
grandpop's bottle
in a belt-pouch
I tried karate
on Johanna Iscobwitz
pregnant, lying down
Her identity
on television
Blood on her
testifying lips
Inside the photo-album
a subversive rhythm

Itzhak's career—
a mumbling pain
At night you would see
Itzhak's non-event
Jelly-roll Morton
was a storyteller
whispering premonitions
of burnt bones
Juxtapositions
to clear the sinuses
of prophets
A wave of groping jobless
immigrants
babyish broken voices
singing "Sweet Lorraine"

Hop-a-long grandpop
Everybody's ready
for his flood o' jokes
He explains the romanesque
arches & the billowing
angels o' Sacré Coeur

Young women
listen to a new
fabulous version
of romantic jazz

Women made pottery nudes
with photo-realistic
genitals

Grandpop never took
an atheistic position
never beat his children
never became
a car-thief like
a son-in-law
Grandma.   I write songs

about her
The variety is my
theory of poetry

The first glimpse
of things,
sand, the part
major, the
DNA

In lower Brooklyn
there are some fine
old buildings
I think about the
gravitational effect,
a galaxy of grain molecules
Brooklyn turf Odessa
The surface of sky
Sacré Coeur

I verify the doctrine
I command the grass,
my foot
I am the peasant
eating the cheese,
watching grandma dancing
on the stones of
the parthenon

The problem. The answer
is the organized puzzling
energy

They told grandma
that she was not serious
They removed her skullcap

The second coming,
her tall cerebral grand-

daughter
Expert in juggling acts
From Egypt from Egypt
the land here & there
Shocks of the first
struggle
That sent the word
blazing

Yesterday I hid a
gallon of ship's oil
Pressure forced me
to consider recognition,
sympathy, the Domes
o' Sacré Coeur

Everything I put
There is no shortage
down makes sense
In harmony
with the skeletal
growth

I fight a different enemy
this millenium
The perversity of crisis
Night of new contrasts
Sunlight & Mayan dreams
Erotic, vivid woman's face
The blending of lights
at ten p.m.
Le Flore
C'est soir

13

I am Hamlet of Brooklyn
I want someone
to kiss my hands
I demand the processes
of work
I hate my fantasies
of a four-mouthed reindeer
A spleen transplantation
terrifies me

A shoe-shine boy
sings a song about circles,
economics, and the peeling
walls of lighthouses

A woman falls from the cliff
just below the wind
holding her child like
a rubber plant
In the green wood she passes
the sadist Mengele laughing
at the wooden sticks
on top of Isaac's head
His pockets are stuffed
with credit cards

In a cave of winds
I have revealed my discipline
Later the disentombment
out of the stone
I am the engineer
with a star on my brow

Listen to the scope
of my breath
This is my litany

I advance step by step
Up the hill to Sacré Coeur
Up the hill to Sacré Coeur
wearing ceramic earrings
with tiny pictures
of the Bahamas & West Indies
Islands that can drive you
insane
The austere sun burlesques
my gold dress
I am light & heat

At the vestibule of Sacré Coeur
the silence, I squint my eyes
sharpening the forms
of vast light
I think of the history
of siphoned gas,
soft walls within belief
I hurl the javelin to the top

from

How Much Paint Does the Painting Need

(1988)

Configurations

The blind   said Saud   The blind listen to a pulsebeat
Soundlessly white searches   breaking with things   the spherical
mass   the dislocated target   the configurations   to the edge
of the canvas   maneuvers   rotates   crisscrosses in front of
the blind   the diameter breaks soundlessly its spherical
mass shakes side to side   back to back   front to front
The white target heats-up searching   for blackness   forces
the patterns to the edge   forces itself dead-center   clutches
the hidden recesses of the fibers   whines to a halt   diminishes
The fragments roll   to the edge   back to back   front to front
disrupts the mind of the blind   said Saud

While manic activity took revenge Toulouse twisted
his body for a superior view of cinnamon freckled dancers'
legs   While her tiny mouth tasted wrath   liquid
adherent covering spread on canvas
While pink & black pigment fornicated Toulouse etched the cruelest
slanting-celtic eyes   While the flakes of a
pulverized substance sprinkled his orthopedic shoes wrath
burnt the aorta of Jane   While rapture flowed out
in the muted tangerine-wash   his upward gazing-yearning
Toulouse only saw himself   While he deformed
her nostrils twisting one orifice higher than a gargoyle's
snout   scratching the legs of spiders around her lips
a percentage mark in a diseased skull   Toulouse
only heard himself   only smelled himself   only touched
himself   only ate himself   & that's what Jane
felt

The sound of the buzz-saw was
making her apprehensive   the story of   popping noises
Like Saud she dyed her hair bright red   always smiling
rubbing her foot on a little dog   everywhere I stand is
enemy territory   my eyesight is that of a saber-toothed tiger
she mumbled   flushing sickly   The buzz-saw causes her
to turn   in the way of the sound Saud invented
Watching the fog over the pond she pushes back
her chair to rise   She giggles in her dream   seeing Martin
Luther form a curvy shape in the air with his hands pointing
in her direction   Brushing her bright red hair
the little dog leaps up to bite her calf

Now you sound like a woman   said Saud
from my country   a chummy relationship   you'll cook meals
for my friends   sooner or later   you'll be piercing
your ears   infecting your lobes   flushing rusty-orange
menstrual pads down the toilet   stupidly putting
nectarine pits in the air-conditioner unit   buying leather
sandals   in all the colors of the rainbow   sneakily
rubbing peanut oil into your abdominal scar
Your baggy crotch   lilac-satin   harem pajamas   a daily
erotic ballad in my life   O that I might stay
in your country   finishing up my orals   like a thief
in the night   like a singing cowboy

I was inspired   by   the upward rolling eye
no one saw me   moving closer   to the stage   to ogle
almost to the edge   an image of a Cretan maiden wearing
black spider-web stockings leaping on a bull   She had
mouthed the words   a wreath for Toulouse   laurel
of course   she said   I laughed   a cripple in love with
a cabaret dancer   Standing near a wash basin & a tank
with a spigot   & a mass of metal cast leavings
I saw myself   applying red paint   in intersecting
circles   her transparent-celtic eyes turning
cold blue-green   as I   humbly   make paint to her

Examine variously the scratch-marked syphilitic nose
of the head of a king   said Saud   Hairs ejected
from the pores   meandering continuous
whorls of wiry hairs   wiry hairs
whorls of scratch-marks meandering   Whole surfaces etched
cancerous on the face   artificial ruptures ejecting
madrigals of pus   The king's pristine scrotum   bellows Saud
gives content & structure to the romance & reality
of the middle ages   He was a fighter & a lover
but coldly rejected   smiles Saud
He was a fighter & a lover   my brother & my mother
ejecting madrigals of pus   White eyelashes   artificial lines
screams Saud   I'll take the architecture
You can keep the plague!

She was born in the basil plant
near the exposed recesses   near a system of doubts
maps of non-existent islands   She loved to go to the edge
of things   slipping on rocks   a system of sorrow
bright nuclear reflections   hollow insect black & gold
charred skeletal structures think of slipping on rocks
or laughing up your sleeve   as a door opens
black & gold ravenous insects stare you down   a system
of fear   continuous veins of the basil plant
the dynamic cartilage of the rat's thigh   think
of your sleeve   the hidden recesses born
in the volcano   the hollowness non-descript   depressed
structures exposed like the charred bits of the
rat's thigh   The door opens   you're ravenous   you love
to go   to the edge of things
maps of non-existent islands

O I pressed   my pustules tenderly!   O Slow cruel
rows of fiery pearls   seething swellings
silky protuberances   vengeful flowers
obscene milk-plugs   poisonous berries   spitting hives
gruesome baubles   foul coins   soldier ants   insane dancers
goblins nipples   malodorous crops   humping bumps
festering bulges   diamond buttons of pain
crystal sores   shrieking cysts   hideous groupings
grotesque choirs   venomous assemblies   adders kisses
incestuous families   howling gangs   putrified patterns
etching tormentors   possibilities of   ugliness
that make christian & moslem mothers weep!   O Wash
my pustules in gold!   O Wash my pustules in gold!   & let
the pope's eyelids   encrust with my wounds filth!

She said that she was all tangled impulses   that she would be
made into a monkey   She had seen the monkey
in her eye under the lower lid   She was trying
to remove it   gently   moving her eyelid up & down   to
dislodge the monkey   She felt like a fly in a bottle
The monkey would not budge   The eye became
swollen the lid bulbous & blood-packed   The eye shifted
slightly higher on her face   The monkey lifted
its leg at her   The point is not to disappear in the
chill of autumn   like a leaf on the branch
of a dead tree   The monkey spoke in sign language saying
You said that the soft space   above the corner   of my
lips   was difficult to trace

for: Egon Schiele

She comes out from the black curtain
She says she could see & be able to paint by mouth
She's intoning words: A British flag   a pair of Japanese
dolls   several ceramic pitchers   a toy boat   theatre posters
Confined to her bed   after the accident   she could
paint waterfalls by mouth   horses & pastoral
scenes   scrolls from Tibet   & ominous gloves   She did not
lose her happiness in death & other things various
as the phases of the moon   A woman threading
a needle with her toes in a side-show   The nerves in the
onion-shaped calves spasmodic in the dusk
She practised daily   After two or three months she
began to draw an elongated figure   The brush
would scratch the inside of her mouth

for: Elaine Stoloff Shragge

Her sacrament of thrill under her skin
of the fingertips   as she modeled her first piece of sculpture
a naturalistic head of Emily Dickinson   It had first been
before closing off the ends   of the clay   a thick
head of Marcel Duchamp   but she said Nicht gut to her need
to be accepted by the public   I'm going
to relate to the direction of my voice   relate
my voice   to going   in the direction   of where I'm thinking
I'm tapering   roughing   smoothing   urging on
Olowe the artist's glowing dream-pictures   my polonaise
eye to follow   the skin of the fingertips
shares the expanse   of the f o o t p r i n t s

The pursuit of anatomical correctness
She finds it   a beloved female image   in a chunk of concrete
This light obsessive   gentle   this light remigrating
zigzagging rapidly   continuously working the ridges
of color   tension intertwined with the canvas
climbing onto her back   Her wrist twisted beating
the rapid pulsating mounds of pigment   scooped out of the
matrix   muscle   tissue   fiber   tendons in the wet
surfaces   She felt that she hasn't been able
to paint fast enough   the pressure   to make the haunch
of the bucking bull   more powerful   to enlarge
the gray haunch   dominate the canvas
suck in her genius breath

Going to the edge   laboring the surface
The strangeness & bleakness of black   merging into gray
Tearing into the yellow rhythms   into the emergency
of blue between the bubbles   the spaces burn
break free of the canvas   grafting the nerves onto the
surface   the base of the skull   forged   into the fibers
tearing the canvas   edging into the territory
simply breathing   on the bubbles   going to the surface
between the veins of blue   the pigment forged
into the base   of the skull   the territory breaking
out of the paint   between the spaces   tearing through

Ode to a Tea-Serving Set 1924-1955

They don't give teas anymore   The last tea   was given about
fifteen years ago   It might as well have been fifty   The teas
just simply stopped like my grandfather's clock   When was the
last tea given, I said softly swinging a wine cup of plastic
between three fingers   Fifteen years ago the last tea   was
given fifteen years ago in 1968   They don't give teas
anymore   Fifteen years ago it might as well have been fifty
The rococo-style tea-serving set is owned by the department
of English and entrusted to 'He Who Is The Chair' but it's
the chair's spouse who's obliged to deal with it   Deal with
a tea-serving set?   I said   It can be a burden, you know
Yes, I said   It tarnishes before your very eyes to a purplish
black when it is exposed to air   The last chairman's spouse
had housed the tea-serving set in a glass cabinet

And on a scale of 1 to 10 it gleamed an 8   It was wonderfully
displayed   It never tarnished   And she never gave a tea   They
don't give teas anymore   It was a civilized person who decided
that the words "In memoriam Ernest Carson Ross 1924-1955"
be engraved on two majestic silver platters   And the custom
of tea drinking with its own etiquette and special equipment
would endure   And objects of silver adorning the tea table
would proclaim the status of the English department forever
& forever   Perhaps it was the dead professor's wife or daughter
who felt the silver forms clatter about in her head   To sip
tea & munch buttered scones among style-conscious elite
academicians with spouses   How restful!   But they don't give
teas anymore   It was a civilized person who decided that
the words "in memoriam Ernest Carson Ross 1924-1955" be
engraved on two majestic silver platters   Platters that in
the opinion of some were more suitable to hold a buffalo head

www.ingramcontent.com/pod-product-compliance
Lightning Source LLC
Chambersburg PA
CBHW032127160426
43197CB00008B/542